LifeLight

"In Him was life, and the life was the light of men." John 1:4

Wilderness Wanderings (Leviticus, Numbers, Deuteronomy)

LEADERS GUIDE

I0806854

CONCORDIA PUBLISHING HOUSE • SAINT LOUIS

From lecture one:

A company of around two million people is bound to get mighty hungry! This is especially true as they wander through the barren wilderness, where crop-growing for them will be an absolute impossibility. Trade will be scarce, because they are going to be off the well-worn trading routes that run closer to the shore of the Mediterranean Sea. . . .

He gives the manna in the morning, the quail in the evening in order to awaken and strengthen faith: (Exodus 16:12) "Then you shall know that I am the LORD your God." The verb *know* is an experiential word—as if to say, "They will have proof directly from Me that I actually come through on the promises I make."

The Real Story of the Exodus
by Gerad Taylor © 2009 CPH.

3558 S. Jefferson Ave., St. Louis, MO 63118-3968
1-800-325-3040 • www.cph.org

Written by Mark Stirdivant

Edited by Brian Chisamore

Cover illustration © 2009 CPH/Gerad Taylor

This publication may be available in braille, in large print, or on cassette tape for the visually impaired. Please allow 8 to 12 weeks for delivery. Write to Lutheran Blind Mission, 7550 Watson Rd., St. Louis, MO 63119-4409; call toll-free 1-888-215-2455; or visit the Web site: www.blindmission.org.

Manufactured in the United States of America

1 2 3 4 5 6 7 8 9 10 21 20 19 18 17 16 15 14 13 12

Contents

Introduction

Welcome to LifeLight

A special pleasure is in store for you. You will be instrumental in leading your brothers and sisters in Christ closer to Him who is our life and light (John 1:4). You will have the pleasure of seeing fellow Christians discover new insights and rediscover old ones as they open the Scriptures and dig deep into them, perhaps deeper than they have ever dug before. More than that, you will have the pleasure of sharing in this wonderful study.

LifeLight—An In-depth Study

LifeLight is a series of in-depth Bible studies. The goal of LifeLight is that through a regular program of in-depth personal and group study of Scripture, more and more Christian adults may grow in their personal faith in Jesus Christ, enjoy fellowship with the members of His body, and reach out in love to others in witness and service.

In-depth means that this Bible study includes the following four components: individual daily home study; discussion in a small group; a lecture presentation on the Scripture portion under study; and an enhancement of the week's material (through reading the enrichment magazine).

LifeLight Participants

LifeLight participants are adults who desire a deeper study of the Scriptures than is available in the typical Sunday morning adult Bible class. (Mid-to-older teens might also be LifeLight participants.) While LifeLight does not assume an existing knowledge of the Bible or special experience or skills in Bible study, it does assume a level of commitment that will bring participants to each of the nine weekly assemblies having read the assigned readings and attempted to answer the study questions. Daily reading and study will require from 15 to 30 minutes for the five days preceding the LifeLight assembly. The day following the assembly will be spent reviewing the previous week's study by going over the completed study leaflet and the enrichment magazine.

LifeLight Leadership

While the in-depth process used by LifeLight begins with individual study and cannot achieve its aims without this individual effort, it cannot be completed by individual study alone. Therefore, trained leaders are necessary. You fill one or perhaps more of the important roles described below.

The Director

This person oversees the LifeLight program in a local center (which may be a congregation or a center operated by several neighboring congregations). The director

- serves as the parish LifeLight overall coordinator and leader;
- coordinates the scheduling of the LifeLight program;
- orders materials;
- convenes LifeLight leadership-team meetings;
- develops publicity materials;
- recruits participants;
- maintains records and budgeting;
- assigns, with the leadership team, participants to small discussion groups;
- makes arrangements for facilities;
- communicates outreach opportunities to small-group leaders and to congregational boards;
- follows up on participants who leave the program.

The Assistant Director *(optional)*

This person may assist the director. Duties listed for the director may be assigned to the assistant director as mutually agreeable.

The Lecture Leader

This person prepares and delivers the lecture at the weekly assembly. **(Lesson material for the lecture leader begins on p. 8.)** The lecture leader

- prepares and presents the Bible study lecture to the large group;

- prepares worship activities (devotional thought, hymn, prayer), using resources in the study leaflet and leaders guide and possibly other, outside sources;
- helps the small-group discussion leaders to grow in understanding the content of the lessons;
- encourages prayer at weekly leadership-team and discussion-leaders meetings.

The Small-Group Coordinator *(optional; the director may fill this role)*

This person supervises and coordinates the work of the small-group discussion leaders. The small-group coordinator

- recruits with the leadership team the small-group discussion leaders;
- trains or arranges for training of the discussion leaders;
- assists the director and discussion leaders in follow-up and outreach;
- encourages the discussion leaders to contact absent group members;
- participates in the weekly leadership-team and discussion-leaders equipping meetings;
- provides ongoing training and support as needed.

The Small-Group Discussion Leaders

These people guide and facilitate discussion of LifeLight participants in the small groups. **(Lesson material for the small-group leaders begins on p. 53.)** There should be one discussion leader for every group of no more than twelve participants. The small-group discussion leaders are, perhaps, those individuals who are most important to the success of the program. They should, therefore, be chosen with special care and be equipped with skills needed to guide discussion and to foster a caring fellowship within the group. These discussion leaders

- prepare each week for the small-group discussion by using the study leaflet and small-group leaders guide section for that session **(see p. 53)**;
- read the enrichment magazine as a study supplement;
- guide and facilitate discussion in their small group;
- encourage and assist the discussion group in prayer;
- foster fellowship and mutual care within the discussion group;
- attend weekly discussion leaders training meetings.

Leadership Training

LifeLight leaders will meet weekly to review the previous week's work and plan the coming week. At this session, leaders can address concerns and prepare for the coming session. LifeLight is a 1½-hour program with no possibility for it to be taught in the one hour typically available on Sunday mornings. Some congregations, however, may want to use the Sunday morning Bible study hour for LifeLight preparation and leadership training. In such a meeting, the lecture leader and/or small-group coordinator may lead the discussion leaders through the coming week's lesson, reserving 5 or 10 minutes for problem solving or other group concerns.

While it requires intense effort, LifeLight has proven to bring great benefit to LifeLight participants. The effort put into this program, both by leaders and by participants, will be rewarding and profitable.

The LifeLight Weekly Schedule

Here is how LifeLight will work week by week:

1. Before session 1, each participant will receive the study leaflet for session 1 and the enrichment magazine for the course. The study leaflet contains worship resources (for use both in individual daily study and at the opening of the following week's assembly) and readings and study questions for five days. Challenge questions will lead those participants who have the time and desire a greater challenge into even deeper levels of study.

2. After the five days of individual study at home, participants will gather for a weekly assembly of all LifeLight participants. The assembly will begin with a brief period of worship (5 minutes). Participants will then join their assigned small discussion groups (of twelve or fewer, who will remain the same throughout the course), where they will go over the week's study questions together (55 minutes). Assembling together once again, participants will listen to a lecture presentation on the readings they have studied in the previous week and discussed in their small groups (20 minutes). After the lecture presentation, the director or another leader

will distribute the study leaflet for the following week. Closing announcements and other necessary business may take another five minutes before dismissal.

In some places some small groups will not join the weekly assembly because of scheduling or other reasons. Such groups may meet at another time and place (perhaps in the home of one of the small group's members). Those congregations may record the lecture given by the lecture leader at the weekly assembly and duplicate it for use by other groups meeting later in the week.

3. On the day following the assembly, participants will review the preceding week's work by rereading the study leaflet they completed (and that they perhaps supplemented or corrected during the discussion in their small group) and by reading appropriate articles in the enrichment magazine.

Then the LifeLight weekly study process will begin all over again!

Recommended Study Resources and Worship

The Lutheran Study Bible. St. Louis: Concordia Publishing House, 2009. This resource contains more than 26,000 study and application notes, a most thorough reference guide (pp. lxv-cx), and over 90,000 cross-references, as well as a 31,000-entry concordance, maps, charts, and timelines.

Roehrs, Walter R., and Martin H. Franzmann. *Concordia Self-Study Commentary*. St. Louis: Concordia Publishing House, 1979. This one-volume commentary on the Bible contains 950 pages and is tailored for lay use.

The Concordia Organist is a 31-CD collection of pipe organ accompaniments for all the hymns and liturgical music in *Lutheran Service Book*. St. Louis: Concordia Publishing House (order no. 99-2264). Use these CDs for worship hymn accompaniment.

Kleinig, John W. *Concordia Commentary: Leviticus*. St. Louis: Concordia Publishing House, 2003. An in-depth look into the Book of Leviticus.

How Did We Get Here?

Exodus; Numbers 7–9; 11; 13–14; Deuteronomy 5–8

Preparing for the Session

Central Focus

This session serves as an introduction to the wilderness wanderings of the Israelites, touching briefly on the exodus from Egypt and setting the stage for the forty years that follow it. Given this context, a clearer light can then shine upon the last three Books of Moses.

Objectives

That participants, led by the Holy Spirit working through God's Word, will

1. review the exodus and the actions of the Israelites immediately following;
2. take note of the significance of these early events to the current study; and
3. be able to relate these events to further study of Leviticus, Numbers, and Deuteronomy.

Note for the small-group leaders: Lesson notes and other materials you will need begin on page 54.

For the Lecture Leader

Session Plan

Worship

Begin the session with the hymn printed in the study leaflet. Accompaniments are available in denominational hymnals, such as *Lutheran Service Book* or *Lutheran Worship* (refer to hymnal index). (Note: Concordia Publishing House has available *The Concordia Organist.* All the initial worship hymns in the LifeLight courses are included in this resource. It's especially helpful for mission congregations and small parishes. See the list of study resources on page 7.) Follow with this prayer:

Prayer

O Lord, who has called us out of darkness into Your marvelous light, we pray for the light of truth that only You can reveal to us. Open Your Holy Word to us and grant us the insight of the Holy Spirit so that we may use that Word to grow in faith toward You and love toward our neighbor. As we follow Your ancient people Israel into the wilderness during their forty years of wandering, guide us also with Your powerful hand, dealing with us not after our sins but according to Your mercy in Christ. Amen.

Lecture Presentation

1 Beginning at the Exodus (skim Exodus 12; Numbers 9)

Welcome to the wilderness! While the scriptural account of forty years of Israelite wandering is often considered "flyover" country in the world of Bible study, it is still a significant event in God's unfolding of His salvation history in the Old Testament. One's tendency is to skip all of the endless details in the books of Leviticus, Numbers, and Deuteronomy on one's way from the mighty exodus events to the battles of Joshua in the Promised Land. All those who have ever committed themselves to read the entire Bible cover to cover can attest that there is some difficult material here to trudge through. I recall the idea that King Xerxes had, as told in the Book of Esther: he couldn't sleep one night, so he commanded the royal record of detailed minutes to be read to him. That would probably be how lots of frustrated Bible readers would approach the last three books of the Pentateuch—as a cure for insomnia!

But the wilderness wanderings writings *are*, in fact, important. This is especially the case when considering the role these books play linking the classic Old Testament watershed salvation event that occurred in Egypt with the realization of the ancient divine promise upon the crossing of the Jordan River. In their extended period of traversing the desert, God's chosen people were given a lesson to learn about their Creator and the all-important promise of a Savior that they had received from their ancestors. Many of them did not believe, and so their bones lay scattered about the desolate terrain. Others were overcome with the difficult trials that accompanied this wandering, so that both the past deliverance and the future promise had faded in their spiritual consciousness. Roaming the wilderness was certainly not going to be easy for them.

You could say, perhaps, that we have a similar "in-between" time that we experience today, with the complete salvation already accomplished by our Lord on the cross behind us, and His glorious, heavenly final coming still ahead. Jesus is no mere footnote or interesting detail in our history! Nor is He simply a source of valuable wisdom on which we can rely to bring us worldly success. He is our guide on the journey that leads to heaven, that is, our final promised land. He is present with us in His glorified, divinely human flesh. And, just like the Israelites in the wilderness, though on earth we have no abiding city, we are moving forward toward that city that will last forever, in which we will meet the Lord face-to-face, just as a person would meet with a friend.

First, we ask as we gaze at the wilderness about us, how did we get here? What is the great event of salvation that determines our very identity? For the original wilderness wanderers, it was the exodus—the mass exit of hundreds of thousands of people, along with their possessions and animals, out of Egypt and into the remote and forbidding Sinai Peninsula. Imagine the entire city of Paris picking up and moving out of France! And not only that, but this humongous community-in-transit, which once dwelled in the fertile area fed by the unique Nile lifeline, was now headed for a land that, in comparison, had little to offer in the way of supporting resources.

Clearly, this trip to the Promised Land was going to require massive faith on the part of the Israelites. This faith was not going to originate within their own hearts, but rather it would be planted there by the gracious, yet powerful, finger of God Himself. They had witnessed the mighty plagues that the Lord unleashed on Pharaoh and the people of Egypt. They had received an enormous wealth of their captors' goods simply because God had made the Egyptians "favorably disposed" toward them. Finally, they were rescued through the waters of the Red Sea, which were the very same waters that decisively decimated the forces that were determined to yoke them into slavery. Now that they were all to themselves in the Sinai wilderness, they saw the Lord's guiding presence accompanying them in the pillar of cloud. These events, taken together, are part of what Paul writes about when he speaks of the Israelites being "baptized into Moses" (1 Corinthians 10:2).

The Christian Church takes part in her own mighty deliverance—the death and resurrection of Jesus—through Baptism. Just as the wandering Israelites were referred back to what God did for them in leaving Egypt, we are helped in our spiritual journey by a constant remembrance of our living Savior. As we follow this traveling nation in their forty-year episode across the span of three biblical books, we will find how our own spiritual walk is strengthened by the comforting presence of our Lord who delivered us from the bondage of our sins.

2 Promise of Canaan (Exodus 23:20–33; Numbers 13–14)

Somewhere along the way, Moses was inspired to write the Book of Genesis, and I have no doubt that this essential history was read to the Israelites so that they would recall God's ancient promise to their ancestor Abraham. This man, himself merely a "wandering Aramean" (Deuteronomy 26:5) like his grandson Jacob after him, had faced a great crisis in his life. His brother Haran died back at home, and his orphaned nephew Lot came along as they set out together on the westward journey. Abraham made his way up along the Euphrates River, headed for the land of Canaan. When his father Terah died, Abraham was at a personal crossroads. Do I go back home to Ur? Do I stay where I am at this in-between place of Haran? Or do I press on and head for Canaan? It was at that precise moment in Abraham's life that the Lord stepped in.

Abraham didn't pray for guidance. He wasn't fishing around for contact with the Almighty God. Instead, the Lord chose him and spoke His everlasting promise to him. Abraham was not a great nation when he first received the divine promise. He had no one who would carry on after him. But the Lord bound Himself with an oath to Abraham, purely by grace, that He would give this lonely traveler two great gifts: descendants and land (Genesis 15). Both of these blessings were going to demand an impossible feat to accomplish, humanly speaking.

As you may recall, Abraham and Sarah were childless until Isaac was born to them while they were in their nineties. The Lord performed that which man says is impossible. The promised multitude of descendants would come in due time. When Abraham entered the land of his inheritance, several different strong, well-established nations were already there. How could he root them out single-handedly? Impossible, it seemed. For the time being, Abraham and his family's next two generations simply lived in tents (Hebrews 11:9) side by side with these larger peoples and cities. The time to cleanse the land and claim the Lord's promise would also come when He determined.

Finally, when the 430 years in Egypt came to their completion, to the very day (Exodus 12:40–41), the multitude of Abraham's descendants began their journey to fulfill his promised inheritance. They had the bones of Joseph in tow, keeping in mind this family hero's firm faith in the completion of God's Word. Incidentally, he could have directed his family members to make a special funeral trip from Egypt to the family grave site and back again, just as he did upon the death of his father, Jacob. It makes you wonder if Joseph perhaps wanted to wait to have his body buried until it all would come true as the Lord had said. He wanted to participate, you could say, with his bones at least, in the great salvation event that the Holy Spirit allowed him to foresee (Genesis 50:25; Exodus 13:19).

Wandering in the wilderness was never considered as the final goal of the exodus. As Moses dutifully records Israel's civil and ceremonial laws the first time around on Mount Sinai, it was clear from the very start that the conquest and settlement of Canaan was considered a done deal from the perspective of Almighty God. (Exodus 23:23–25) "When . . . I blot them out"—the current inhabitants of the Promised Land, that is—do "not bow down to their gods nor serve them. . . . You shall serve the Lord your God." The First Commandment must rule their mind and heart. If not, they lose faith, and they reject the blessing and privilege of being God's chosen people. They reject their Savior even before the time comes for Him to die on the cross for them. Will they listen to the Lord? Or will they listen to frightened spies and distrust Him who brought them out with His all-powerful hand? Those who failed the test would not survive the forty years of wandering in the wilderness. Those who believed the Lord would realize the inauguration of His inheritance that He had promised to Father Abraham.

3 Manna and Water (skim Exodus 16–17; Numbers 11)

A company of around two million people is bound to get mighty hungry! This is especially true as they wander through the barren wilderness, where crop-growing for them will be an absolute impossibility. Trade will be scarce, because they are going to be off the well-worn trading routes that run closer to the shore of the Mediterranean Sea. And whenever you think of a desert, you think of water, or rather, the lack of it. A well could be dug, but that doesn't serve a nation that is collectively on the move. This is going to be a real problem, to say the least, for Moses, the leader of this hungry and thirsty multitude.

The growling stomachs produce the grumbling mouths, and Moses and Aaron point out in frustration, (Exodus 16:8) "Your grumbling is not against us but against the Lord." Again, the lack of faith is the real issue. God would take care of them physically either way, because it remains true that He "makes His sun rise on the evil and on the good, and sends rain on the just and on the unjust" (Matthew 5:45). The grumbling is what catches the Lord's attention—this is not an example of praying in confident faith. This is instead a serious doubt that the heavenly Father is gracious and merciful, abounding in steadfast love and faithfulness to His people. He gives the manna in the morning, the quail in the evening in order to awaken and strengthen faith: (Exodus 16:12) "Then you shall know that I am the Lord your God." The verb *know* is an experiential word—as if to say, "They will have proof directly from Me that I actually come through on the promises I make." For believers, that knowledge is saving faith that rejoices in God's love and receives His provision of daily bread with thanksgiving. For those who reject Him, this direct contact is not going to be pleasant, as in the case of Pharaoh's army in Exodus 14:18, for example.

The water that God grants in the wilderness (Exodus 17) not only quenches the thirst of the children of Israel in the desert but is also a spiritual drink accompanying these wandering travelers. As Paul points out in the beginning of 1 Corinthians 10, the Red Sea event, along with the giving of the Law on Mount Sinai, was for the ancient forefathers a baptism "into Moses." The spiritual drink came from "the spiritual Rock that followed them, and the Rock was Christ" (v. 4). Moses strikes this rock the first time with his staff, at the command of the Lord, who was standing there before them all. (The second time [Numbers 20:2–13], Moses was told only to speak to the rock, but he failed to do so). From this "stricken rock with streaming side" (*LSB* 534:4), flowed water to save their physical lives, and Christ the spiritual Rock answered affirmatively with His gracious presence the all-important question on the lips of God's people, "Is the LORD among us or not?" (Exodus 17:7).

Now, when you're gathering manna and quail six days a week, and eating it seven days, before long, all your recipes are going to be exhausted! Despite the harsh slavery that they experienced in Egypt, its cucumbers, leeks, onions, garlic, and melons nevertheless started sounding really good in comparison with this monotonous, flaky bread that they picked up off the desert floor. So in Numbers 11, the people are "rewarded," so to speak, for their complaining with the meat that they had demanded, but along with that came the plague that God sent to shock them back, not into utter fealty and abject submission, but into honest repentance and faith in the Lord's unbounded mercy.

4 The Cloudy, Fiery Pillar and the Tabernacle (skim Exodus 13; 26; 40; Numbers 7–9)

These forty years, the manna and quail would follow the children of Israel wherever they went, but there was yet another constant companion, and that was the presence of the Lord Himself. The pillar of cloud by day and the pillar of fire by night showed up right at the very beginning of the journey. This is known in biblical studies as a *theophany*, an instance of God revealing Himself so that He can be seen. More than merely some celestial drum major or night-light, this was the Creator of heaven and earth showing up on the scene to make salvation happen for His people. In this form, the Lord repelled Pharaoh's army so that the chosen people could pass between the waves. Whenever the cloud picked up and moved on, Israel picked up and moved on. Moses would approach this cloud to speak with the Most High, and its divine brightness lit up his face.

However, the pillar of cloud and fire were not intended to be the Lord's self-appointed gracious presence all by themselves. The theophany, sometimes described in Scripture as "the glory of the LORD," would rest on a particular place to which the sinner would go and receive the necessary reconciliation with God and with his neighbor. The same vision that would fill the temple at Solomon's dedication and at Isaiah's commission also appeared to Ezekiel in the land of exile, and finally enshrouded Jesus and the three disciples on the Mount of Transfiguration; this glory vision would inhabit a tent in the middle of this wandering camp. Particular materials and measurements given at Mount Sinai dictated a precise theology of worship: this is all about the Lord's gracious service to His people. Not everybody could come as near as they wanted—only the priests could approach on behalf of all the people.

The tabernacle was the inner tent at the nerve center of Israel's worship—it housed the ark of the covenant, the "testimony" to the Lord's faithful works for His people. Over the tabernacle was a larger tent, the "tent of meeting," in front of which the priests would offer their regular sacrifices. The exception of the Day of Atonement will come up in a more focused discussion later. This tent and tabernacle were situated inside a larger consecrated area known as the "court." Every tribe had its assigned place surrounding it, just as it would have a designated area once the multitude arrived in the Promised Land.

Throughout the years of wandering, the story of the Israelites centered on this quarter-acre complex. Numbers 4 and 10 painstakingly list the necessary steps to follow as the tribal camps take down all the pieces and get them ready for transport before they set out. Note the priority of the tribe of Judah, the tribe of the lineage of Christ. The Kohathites, the men of the tribe of Levi who would be entrusted with carrying this holy centerpiece, would be nestled in the middle of the travelers. They were allowed to carry the ark and all the other furnishings of the sanctuary, but never to touch them—their cousins, the priests who are sons of Aaron, were the ones set aside to do that as they covered everything in preparation for travel. These details were not arbitrary, but rather they impressed upon God's people that His gracious presence in their midst is not a freebie. Rather, this close contact with the holy and almighty God came to them by faith in the one sacrifice toward which all of these symbols point, the all-availing sacrifice of Jesus Christ.

5 Covenant and Ten Commandments (Exodus 20; Deuteronomy 5–8)

In the ancient Hebrew language, the phrase used for making a covenant is *karath berith* (kah-RAHTH buh-REETH), which is literally translated as "*cut* a covenant." The account of the covenant that God made with Abraham in Genesis 15 is quite explicit in detailing the process of cutting apart certain animals so that the covenanting parties may walk in the midst of them in order to seal the contract. As we noted earlier, the fiery cloud of God's presence *alone* passed between the pieces of the animals while Abraham looked on, signaling that this was the Lord's unilateral gift to His people through their revered patriarch.

However, this one-sided testament sworn by the mouth of the Lord Himself does not imply that there is no obligation on the part of believers. It simply means that Almighty God's grace is for us to receive, not for us to demand as though He owed salvation and eternal life to us as our due. This distinction is helpful for us to keep in mind as we delve through the vast array of commandments, statutes, ceremonies, and cases that are found in this extended section of the Pentateuch. If a simplistic Law-and-Gospel comparison were to be done with each verse standing alone out of context, then the Bible student would be disappointed at the overwhelming Law content that is found. As a result, these books will be closed and unable to reveal Christ to the reader. Looking for Law and Gospel is to be encouraged, for sure, but the key is to understand what the Lord is doing in giving these laws to Moses and the children of Israel.

The covenant is not to be considered as a barter agreement between two parties—it truly is a testament in which God announces His sole act of grace for the sake of unworthy sinners. As a confession of faith in the truth that the Lord has revealed, the people respond in the appropriate ways that He outlines in these books. Moses is instructed to keep a meticulous eye on the details, not only to compel the people to realize that they are utterly lost and condemned sinners, but also (and especially) to point the repentant believer constantly to Jesus, the Messiah. That understanding will be useful as we fit the covenant and Ten Commandments in with all the other laws and directions that we'll study in the coming weeks.

This could have been one of the aims when Moses restated on the doorstep of Canaan "all that the Lord had given him" (Deuteronomy 1:3) when the Israelites were still at Mount Sinai. Of course, this "second-giving of the law" (*Deutero-nomos* is Greek for "second-law," hence, "Deuteronomy") was meant for a new generation, a people who had survived the deaths of those who rebelled against the Lord in the wilderness. What Moses wanted to make crystal clear to them, before he drops back and lets the people go with Joshua into the Promised Land, is that faith is not in the actions, rules, and ceremonies, but rather it is centered on the Lord and what He has done. The results of faith on the part of the believer should not be confused with the mighty acts of salvation that are the true decisive elements in the Israelite covenant.

Conclusion

This review has been intended to help give context to the Books of Leviticus, Numbers, and Deuteronomy, as we consider them in the rest of this study. Taken only by themselves, there might have been a greater risk that they would be mistaken as disjointed sets of rules and a hodge-podge of curious stories. Since the Israelites were not plopped into the wilderness out of the sky, this past week of introduction should help us understand the rest of their adventures that we'll address in the sessions to come.

Concluding Activities

Speak a closing prayer, make any necessary announcements, and distribute study leaflet 2.

Making Offerings

Leviticus 1–5; Numbers 28–29

Preparing for the Session

Central Focus

Leviticus begins right away with an in-depth look at the worship life of God's people in the Old Testament. The various offerings that are prescribed at the beginning of the book provide a constant reminder of our total dependence on our merciful, heavenly Father.

Objectives

That participants, led by the Holy Spirit working through God's Word, will

1. identify and differentiate five particular offerings described in Leviticus;
2. find how these offerings fit in to the Lord's ceremonial worship plan of the Old Testament; and
3. relate these offerings to their fulfillment in Christ and the New Testament.

Note for the small-group leaders: Lesson notes and other materials you will need begin on page 58.

For the Lecture Leader

Session Plan

Worship

Begin the session with the hymn printed in the study leaflet. Accompaniments are available in denominational hymnals, such as *Lutheran Service Book* or *Lutheran Worship* (refer to hymnal index). (Note: Concordia Publishing House has available *The Concordia Organist*. All the initial worship hymns in the LifeLight courses are included in this resource. It's especially helpful for mission congregations and small parishes. See the list of study resources on page 7.) Follow with this prayer:

Prayer

Almighty God, You are pleased with the offerings and worship of lowly men because of the perfect sacrifice of Christ. Grant us humble faith to offer before You our sincerest thanks and praise so that we may not fall to the temptation to take Your love for granted. As we see the various offerings presented to You by the children of Israel, make our lives as a pleasing aroma before Your presence and a worthy confession of what our Lord has done for us. In His name we pray. Amen.

Lecture Presentation

1 Burnt Offerings (Leviticus 1; Numbers 28:1–10)

Understanding the Book of Leviticus is all about keeping its context in mind. The book does not appear from out of nowhere. Its directions on the Divine Service that will involve the priests (the members of the tribe of *Levi*, from which the book gets its name) come as a consequence of the inauguration of the tabernacle and the tent of meeting as a place for God to meet with His people in the Divine Service. In Exodus, the story was all about getting to Mount Sinai and Moses beginning to talk to the Lord. Now that we've gotten to Leviticus, the Lord is seen speaking from His new location of gracious presence for the sake of His chosen and redeemed people. He is still speaking to Moses, the author of these first five books of the Bible, but now all of the Israelite people, and not just the priests, will be in earshot of the plans that will be drawn up for their worship of God, and for their growth in faith. Therefore, these liturgical directions build on the relationship that has already been created by the heavenly Father's saving hand, as witnessed in the events of Exodus that we reviewed last week.

Directions on personal burnt offerings start off the Lord's prescribed liturgical rubrics. Right away, we see the repetitive pattern that is set up and will continue for the rest of the book. Dr. John Kleinig, a Lutheran pastor and professor from Australia, and author of *Concordia Commentary: Leviticus*, observes that Leviticus is a practical book, like a manual, rather than a theoretical textbook (*Leviticus*, pp. 4–5). That is to say, it contains very little description of God and of His involvement in Israel's history. The Holy Spirit has already defined these theological points in Genesis and Exodus. Later books, including the New Testament Book of Hebrews, will take on the task of explaining the sacrifices' significance. Instead of these objectives, Leviticus is meant simply to set forth the Lord's chosen process by which He interacts with His people and how they are brought into communion with Him.

The burnt offering is truly a bloody business, and we might as well start our study with it and get used to reading about this practice that seems so archaic and even a little superstitious to us modern people. Fewer and fewer of us these days will have had any substantial experience on a farm or ranch, and so the life and death of animals is largely removed from our consciousness. Perhaps you have heard, or even said, something like, "I know my meat comes from a store wrapped up in paper or plastic; anything beyond that I leave to the experts!" When we read about what is done to animals in books like Leviticus, we automatically think of our beloved pets, and our gut wrenches when we consider these "innocent bystanders" undergoing the graphic violence that God is requiring His people to commit.

If that isn't bad enough, the one offering the sacrifice doesn't simply hand over the animal to the priestly "experts" to let them do all the "dirty work." The offering bearer, for instance, walks his perfect, unblemished bull toward the bronze altar that is standing in front of the tabernacle, lays his hand on the head of the animal and himself slits its throat to kill it. The priest certainly is there to help out, catching the blood in a bowl so that it can be thrown against the side of the altar, but that last close bond is made between owner and animal as the one life is taken so that the other life is spared. What an image to carry with you! What an insight into a blood-bought forgiveness of sins. You could think about rituals like this one as you sing to Jesus in the Lententide hymn "Not All the Blood of Beasts": (*LSB* 431:3) "My faith would lay its hand On that dear head of Thine, While as a penitent I stand, And there confess my sin." Now you know who it is who is the real offering!

2 Grain Offerings (Leviticus 2; Numbers 28:11–15)

Not all of the sacrifices were bloody! Some of them involved the fruits of the field, and they were prepared for sacrifice in a variety of ways, as Leviticus 2 describes. There is, however, some similarity that you can make with the animal sacrifices that were offered: specifically, that the grain offering had to be from the firstfruits. This means that the grain was recently harvested, and before there was any other common, everyday use, the first and best was taken off the top and offered to the Lord. Just as the male lamb, bull, or goat had to be unblemished, without anything that would make it undesirable for use or for food, so also the grain was not to be picked up off of the ground, or reaped from diseased plants, or the product of any other kind of afterthought.

Do you remember Cain in Genesis 4? He offered a sacrifice of "the fruit of the ground" (v. 3). Yet, the Lord did not have regard, that is, did not accept, his sacrifice. What was wrong with it? Some people think that it was only because Abel had offered a lamb from his flock, so his offering was favored while Cain's was not. But Hebrews 11 helps us figure out the rest of this story, because God had His eye on something other than the offering. Verse 4 says, "By faith Abel offered to God a more acceptable sacrifice than Cain, through which he was commended as righteous, God commending him by accepting his gifts. And through his faith, though he died, he still speaks." So, we learn from this that the offering is accepted on account of the faith of the person bringing the offering. When you understand the role of a sacrifice as an outgrowth of a person's faith and a response of trust in the saving acts of the Lord, then it doesn't seem unusual that an offering can be either a male animal or the firstfruits that are reaped from the field.

Firstfruits are mentioned today among us Christians when the topic of stewardship comes up. We sing, (*LSB* 781:1) "We give Thee but Thine own, Whate'er the gift may be; All that we have is Thine alone, A trust, O Lord, from Thee." Priorities tell us what is most important in our life. An insightful question that a boss can ask an interviewee for a job is "What do you prefer to do on weekends or whenever your schedule is otherwise wide open?" This does not mean that the interviewer is all about probing into minute details about hobbies. With this kind of question, he or she simply wants to discern a potential employee's priorities. Similarly, when we, as a first priority, set aside our offerings to the Lord of our time and talents, along with treasure right off the top, then we confess the biblical truth that all we have belongs to God. He accepts the offering, not because He needs it (see Psalm 50:7–15), but because He desires that first-priority kind of faith that demonstrates full trust in Him for all things. When our hearts become soiled with an inherent self-idolatry that is perhaps mixed with the fear that the Lord will somehow fail to provide for us, then—as the Lord cautioned Cain long ago—(Genesis 4:7) "sin is crouching at the door. Its desire is for you, but you must rule over it."

Most English translations use the term "grain offering" to describe the subject of Leviticus 2. The King James Version and Twenty-First Century King James Version (which is not the same as the New King James) both use the term "meat offering" instead. This is because of the archaic English use of the word *meat* to mean all kinds of food—as in "Thou givest them their meat in due season" (Psalm 145:15 KJV). Since today's readers might find it confusing to come across the word *meat* when Scripture is talking about baking or roasting grain, the Hebrew phrase is most often rendered "grain offering."

Whatever the term, this offering is included among the several that are brought to the priests and are not entirely burned in sacrifice, as opposed to what was commanded in Leviticus 1. A "memorial portion" is dedicated to the Lord, mixed with olive oil, topped with frankincense, and burnt as a "pleasing aroma," but the rest is reserved as a food portion for the priests, the "sons of Aaron," to eat in the courts in front of the tabernacle. In this way, the holy foods are set aside for the holy men, the priests, to eat in the holy place as their day-to-day sustenance for living that has been provided to them by God the Father's grace, as that grace is expressed through the offerings of His holy people.

3 Peace Offerings (Leviticus 3)

Most English translations keep the term "peace offering" when they turn to the sacrificial directions of Leviticus 3. This convention flows quite naturally from the Hebrew word itself, which is related to the well-known noun *shalom*, which is Hebrew for "peace." While the original gives the word in its plural form, so that literally it should read "peace *offerings*," the translations almost always keep it in the singular. Some newer English versions have branched out into different words for this sacrifice, primarily to reflect different shades of meaning that were otherwise overlooked by the old term. The NIV editors chose to use the phrase "fellowship offering" in order to highlight the fact that this gift was given by an individual in order to foster completion or harmony (*shalom*) among the Israelite community. If you consult the New Revised Standard Version, you will find these called "sacrifice of well-being," which further interprets the concept of peace, but perhaps this translation narrows it down too far, so that it would seem to refer only to a psychological peace of mind.

You may find at first some similarities between the peace offerings of chapter 3 and the burnt offerings that are commanded in chapter 1. The directions start with cattle, then sheep and goats. Blood is drained and thrown against the altar. But then the differences start leaping out at you. This time, for the peace offering, both male and female animals are allowed. From the herd, a bull or cow is brought forward; however, the animal must still be without blemish. The same thing goes for the sheep and goats.

Another portion of the animal is brought forward for emphasis in this chapter, and that is the fat. This is not the kind of fat that is found on the meat, but rather it is the fat that is removed along with the animal's inner organs such as the kidneys, liver, and intestines. This fat is more of a milky substance, as the original Hebrew word implies. The ancient world saw this fat as an important food and energy source for the animal, judging perhaps from the way they observed it as it burned. Dr. Kleinig notes, "The fat from an animal had special religious significance. Many pagan religions believed that just as the 'life' of an animal was found in its blood, its spiritual power and strength lay in its fat. Those who ate these parts supposedly gained supernatural power by eating the fat from animals that had been sacrificed to a deity" (*Leviticus*, p. 85). *The Lutheran Study Bible* includes a note on page 168 that the liver of an animal was burned in the peace offering ritual so that it could not be used in fortune-telling and divination, in total opposition to a widely held pagan belief.

As was the case with the burnt offering, the peace offering, including the fat from the animal, was burned on top of the wood that had been ignited on the bronze altar in front of the tent of meeting. The priest was to perform this action, as commanded by the Lord through Moses, following the ceremony in which he threw the blood of the sacrificed animal against the altar. The "pleasing aroma" that is mentioned here is an echo of what was already described in chapter 1. It isn't accurate to say that the burning flesh by itself is pleasing to the Lord, as if He is informing us about a preference or a strange taste of His. Rather, the thing that makes these burnt sacrifices and their strong aromas "pleasing" to God is the solid promise that He has given to His people to believe with a faith that has been created in their hearts by the Holy Spirit. The incense mixed in with the flour of the grain offering would have helped the aroma become a bit more pleasing to those in the courtyard as well!

One phrase that we have seen quite a bit in these first few chapters of Leviticus is "food offering." Some versions, such as the King James, translates this instead as "an offering made by fire." This is because the Hebrew word in question is associated with a word for fire. Recent studies and comparative research with other languages that are similar to Hebrew have brought forward other insights. Kleinig (*Leviticus*, p. 57) suggests that since not all of these offerings are burned (such as the wine in Numbers 15:10), and since not all burnt sacrifices are included in this category, the so-called "food offering" should be considered not as "an offering made by fire," but rather as a gift that is considered as "favorably received by the Lord."

4 Sin Offerings (Leviticus 4; Numbers 29:31–34, 38)

The first time sin is addressed in Leviticus, it is specifically the "unintentional" type of sin. This distinction is made clear by the use of the Hebrew word that technically means "miss the mark." In setting down these regulations, God assumes that He is dealing with His faithful people. He does not naively assume that they will be as perfect and pure as the wind-driven snow, however. He is aware that a hardened, wicked intent would not be constantly driving them away from Him, that is, if they continue in His life-giving and faith-building Word.

As with the first examples of offerings, the sin offering begins with the bigger or more important animals and then proceeds to smaller ones. Since sin affects the very heart of man's relationship with God, more ceremony and detail attends the actions that He deems necessary to clear away that barrier. Again, the section starts with the offering of a young bull, just like what was prescribed for the burnt offering, but this time the bull is meant for an unintentional sin committed by the "anointed" or high priest or by the whole congregation. The priest is held in the same category as the congregation because of the public nature of the office in which he is ordained.

Now that sin is the subject of sacrifice, the priest is required to bring some blood into the very presence of the Lord, that is, into the Holy Place, the tent of meeting in the middle of the court. On the other side of the tabernacle veil with the blood sprinkled in front of it is a smaller altar: this is the gold-covered altar of incense. Only a very small portion of the bull's blood is put on the horns of this altar as an atonement for sin. The rest of the blood is poured out at the base of the bronze altar of burnt offering that sits outside the tabernacle. The fat is burned on the altar, but other parts, namely the skin, dung, legs, and even the head are taken outside the camp to the ash heap to be incinerated.

The goats are used as a sacrifice to cover the unintentional sins of individual people—a male for a leader of a family group, a female for an ordinary member of the Israelites. In this arrangement, you can begin to see a reflection of the order of creation in the ceremonial laws of the Old Testament. A lamb could be substituted for a goat; there is no special distinction there. Whether the sin offering is for a leader or common

this time is not sprinkled, and the priest does not put any blood on the golden altar of incense. Instead, the bronze altar of burnt offering remains the focal point for the atonement of unintentional sins committed by these people. You could imagine the people straining their ears to listen for that oft-repeated and all-important final pronouncement: "and he shall be forgiven."

5 Guilt (or Trespass) Offerings (Leviticus 5)

The procedures for unintentional sin offerings spill over a little bit into chapter 5, but an important distinction is introduced here. So far, the sins addressed have involved an action, even though unintentional, that was committed by the individual who is offering the sacrifice to cover for that sin. There are also sins of omission, that is, where the person should have done something in obedience to God's command, but neglected to do so.

The first example that is offered is a scenario related to the Eighth Commandment. In it, the person has received an official order to testify to a matter—like a subpoena to appear as a witness in court—and he does not. The fault is clearly his, but the offering is still a female lamb or goat, accompanied by his confession of sin, of course. Other cases are covered, such as uncleanness and uttering a rash oath.

At this point, the question may be raised, "Why does Leviticus speak as much as it does about the differences between sins, when it is true from passages like James 2:10 that all sins are equally condemning before God?" To be sure, when placed in relationship to God and

His perfect Law, all sins, no matter what their apparent differences may be to us, are deserving of temporal and eternal punishment. These ceremonial distinctions teach us the valuable lesson that different sins have different effects on our faith and on our relationship with other people. We find ourselves inside the boundaries of the much narrower topic of sanctification (the Christian's holy life of faith), a topic that should have no bearing on whether we have forgiveness or the promise of eternal life, both of which are ours solely by God's grace. And so, while our Lord Jesus Christ has perfectly fulfilled all of God the Father's laws for our justification (or our status as righteous), our Savior has also granted us full sanctification and reconciliation with our fellow human beings. The essential sacrifices, including these unintentional sin offerings, point our attention forward to the cross, where all sin, regardless of differentiation, is destroyed in Christ's once-for-all sacrifice.

The last distinction addressed in this section of Leviticus is the guilt offering. Some Bible versions, such as the King James, call this the "trespass offering." Dr. Kleinig's choice here is "reparation offering" (*Leviticus*, pp. 125–40). While there are several similarities between this and the sin offering, the guilt offering adds a provision for making restitution for the sin that had been unintentionally committed. Even though malicious intent is still not connected with sins of this type, they are a little more serious than those covered by the sin offering. Whereas sin earlier had been characterized as simply "missing the mark," the trespasses here are more serious: a "breach of faith," or a "religious sacrilege." Instances of stealing or ruining someone's property fall into this category, because on top of the confession of the sin, a reparation or compensation also needs to be made. Not only should the entire value of the stolen or damaged item be returned immediately, but a fifth of it should also be added above and beyond its value. Even though this feature is added here in the case of the guilt offering, forgiveness still comes as a result of the atonement that was made on behalf of the penitent, and not on condition of his act of making compensation. That is why we need to make a clear distinction between our atonement on the one hand, which is something God grants us as a gift, and our fruits of repentance on the other hand, which spring forth from the faith that He has planted in our hearts.

Conclusion

The offerings that are described in these first few chapters of Leviticus are required of the people to offer for themselves, rather than sacrifices for the priests to offer in public on behalf of all. As we proceed through the books of the wilderness wanderings, we will come across other regulations that will govern the people as a whole congregation.

Concluding Activities

Speak a closing prayer, make any necessary announcements, and distribute study leaflet 3.

Priestly Ministry

Leviticus 6–10; Numbers 3–4; 12; 15; 18–19; Deuteronomy 12–13

Preparing for the Session

Central Focus

The priests stood between God and men in a complex sacrificial system that was meant to prepare for the coming of Christ. Now that our Savior has completed His saving mission through His death, resurrection, and ascension, we Christians are privileged to identify ourselves as royal priests, offering our spiritual sacrifices by faith in Him.

Objectives

That participants, led by the Holy Spirit working through God's Word, will

1. gain an insight into the Aaronic priesthood and the role of the Levites;
2. appreciate the value of a divinely appointed intermediary priest; and
3. relate the priestly duties described here to our roles today as royal priests of God.

Note for the small-group leaders: Lesson notes and other materials you will need begin on page 62.

For the Lecture Leader

Session Plan

Worship

Begin the session with the hymn printed in the study leaflet. Accompaniments are available in denominational hymnals, such as *Lutheran Service Book* or *Lutheran Worship* (refer to hymnal index). (Note: Concordia Publishing House has available *The Concordia Organist.* All the initial worship hymns in the LifeLight courses are included in this resource. It's especially helpful for mission congregations and small parishes. See the list of study resources on page 7.) Follow with this prayer:

Prayer

Eternal God, You granted Aaron and his priestly sons access to Your earthly throne of grace in order to offer the sacrifice for the sins of the people. Now that You have made all Christians to be Your royal priests, welcome us into Your kingdom and teach us to pray with boldness and confidence, that no adversity in this life may rob us of the promised inheritance that is already ours in the life to come; through Jesus Christ our Lord. Amen.

Lecture Presentation

1 Aaron's Sons and Levites (Leviticus 7; Numbers 3–4)

Moses will be sure to tell you: be careful what you ask for; you just might get it—and not in the way you had originally intended! "Please send someone else!" so Moses pleaded when the Lord commissioned him from the burning bush (Exodus 3), and that "someone else" ended up being his older brother Aaron. But instead of letting Moses off the hook and making Aaron the man in charge of leading the people out of Egypt, God had in mind to keep Moses in the role He had set out for him, and to assign Aaron an important part that perhaps even his brother had not seen coming.

Standing before Pharaoh in Egypt, Aaron's job was to be the mouthpiece for Moses. It sounds a little odd at first, but the Lord described it this way: (Exodus 7:1) "See, I have made you like God to Pharaoh, and your brother Aaron shall be your prophet." All I can think of when I read this verse is the picture of two little brothers putting on robes and playing make-believe church in the house! But together, they went to Pharaoh, thanks to Moses' complaint about his fat lips, considering himself unable to speak clearly (Exodus 6:12). Aaron the prophet was given charge of the staff that Moses had taken in hand on his first visit to Mount Sinai. And as the plagues fell upon Egypt one by one, the team of Moses and Aaron carried out the Lord's will to release His people.

Now that Israel was out in the wilderness, Aaron would receive a modification in his job description. It would seem to be a promotion, given that instead of appearing before a human king who only claimed to be divine, now Moses' big brother would be the only one allowed once a year to appear in the Most Holy Place, that is, the place of the very presence of the one true God. He and his sons were to be inducted into a holy order, selected by the Lord's hand from an already holy people, so that they would be authorized to handle His holy things.

And note the order in which the whole system is laid out. In Exodus, the directions for the tabernacle, altar, and courtyard were given first as the institution of the Old Testament Divine Service. Then, after that, the priests were consecrated as the ones who would be the designated servants tending to the activities concerned with those liturgical spaces. If it had been handed down the other way around, then the priests themselves would have been more important, as though they were the elite gatekeepers of God's grace, and they would have sole dominion over the accoutrements of worship. In fact, that was exactly the wrong understanding in which Aaron attempted to fill a priestly role in the episode of the golden calf (Exodus 32). Such order was not the Lord's idea for coming close to man—rather, that was man's idea to conduct his own worship toward his own flawed concept of the divine. Because the act was a total breach of the Lord's holiness, the whole nation deserved eternal punishment, from which thankfully God chose to redeem His people.

Only Aaron and his sons were going to be allowed to fill the priestly role. The extensive use of genealogies would ensure that this unbroken tradition of succession would be preserved from generation to generation. The rest of the relatives in Aaron's tribe would be known throughout Scripture as the Levites (and those who were in a direct line of succession from him would become the priests). These citizens of Israel would not be given land in Canaan as an inheritance because, as the Lord Himself said to them, "I am your portion and your inheritance among the people of Israel" (Numbers 18:20). Instead of making their own living, they would depend on the rest of the tribes for sustenance, which would come to them by means of offerings that the people would make to the Lord. The Levites would minister before God in a liturgical function, though not as close to the holy things as their cousins the priests would be. They would be required to work and keep watch unassumingly, be subject to the priests' headship, and do their part to preserve the holy integrity of the Divine Service.

2 Tending to the Duties (Leviticus 6; 9; Numbers 18–19)

It's another workday for the priests and Levites as they perform their service before the tabernacle. The people have already come into the courtyard to stand before the bronze altar with their sacrifices. The burnt offerings and sin offerings, guilt offerings, and grain offerings are all taken care of. The part of the Divine Service that everybody else gets to see has finally wrapped up and the people go back home. Now what? That's when the priests and Levites have more work to do, behind the scenes, as it were.

These men who have no homes or inheritances of their own to enjoy are busy tending to the Lord's work in the holy space of His presence. They take care not to let the fire on the altar ever go out—this could be to remind the people of God's constant presence, but practically speaking, the fire is going to be needed for the next round of sacrifices. They have ashes that they need to carry outside the camp to the place where they are dumped out. Some of the offerings they are even commanded to eat. Not the burnt offering—that is ordered to be entirely consumed by the fire. The grain offering, sin offering, peace offering, and guilt offering belong to the priests to eat as their portion, once the designated parts or "memorials" are burned on the altar. The only time these other offerings are burned entirely—and not eaten by the priest—is when any of these are presented to the Lord on behalf of the priest himself. These ceremonial meals are special, because the Levites are commanded to consume them only in the court of the tent of meeting.

These were meals of privilege for this set-aside tribe, especially when you consider that during their time of wandering, the rest of the people did not eat meat more than just a few times each year. Along with this considerable amount of flesh, the best of the firstfruits, the wine, grain, and oil—all the offerings are set forth as their "perpetual due" (Numbers 18:11). This richness that belongs to these holy servants in exchange for their holy work is a reminder that the Lord is their portion and inheritance.

But with the privilege comes great responsibility over against the rest of their countrymen. The Levitical priesthood is repeatedly said to "bear iniquity" for all the people on account of their God-given position. Iniquity is a burden or debt, both a ceremonial and also a spiritual responsibility that must be satisfied in order to be welcomed into God's gracious presence. Forgiveness removes that barrier of iniquity, and the priest is the mediator whom the Lord designated to bridge the gap and reconcile the two who through sin were wrenched apart. Any common person who attempted to come near God's tent, and thus try to steal away the role of His ordained servants, was destined to die.

In the New Testament, the priestly order and Levitical privileges came to an end. Peter describes every baptized Christian as a member of a royal priesthood (1 Peter 2) that far exceeds what was instituted in the past. In place of the Old Testament-era high priest entering a restricted worship space, we now have Christ, who has ascended into heaven itself, having made peace through the blood of His cross (Hebrews 9:24; Colossians 1:20). This means that there is no longer a priestly mediator standing in front of a holy tent, positioning himself between us and God. Our prayers and spiritual sacrifices are presented directly to the Father through Christ. Forgiveness is granted us as our inheritance through the Holy Spirit, who is present in the Word and Sacraments. The pastors serve us these Means of Grace, not to make themselves into a new breed of priestly mediators, but instead because they are Christ's called servants, set aside in a New Testament–style vocation to proclaim the Gospel Word and hand out the gifts of the cross of Jesus.

The Levites and priests at one time were the ones given access to the Father, because they were put in charge of the bulls, goats, birds, sheep, and scented flour that was offered up by the rest of the people. Now that every Christian is a royal priest, we are all granted full access as adopted children of God, a holy people. We are even considered to be His new and truly genuine Israel (Galatians 6:16). Christians are given an inheritance that is not constituted in land or temporal possessions (sounds similar to the Levites, doesn't it?); therefore, we have our sights set on what our Father has promised for us in His unseen, spiritual kingdom.

3 Using the Blood (Leviticus 8:14–30; Deuteronomy 12–13)

It would seem that blood has a way of catching God's attention. Judging from all that is written about it in Scripture, it may well be the part of our human anatomy that concerns Him the most. He could hear the blood of Abel crying out from the ground (Genesis 4:10), and it was the Father's unchangeable will for His eternal Son to put on human flesh just so that He could shed His own blood for the redemption of all mankind.

When the Lord God graciously allowed Noah's ark to rest on the earth after the flood, He gave to all mankind the gift of meat. After He placed the fear of man in every animal, He also sealed His protection upon the blood of man. To be sure, murder is a disobedience of God's commandment, but because it also means the shedding of blood, He is going to have more to say, namely: (Genesis 9:6) "Whoever sheds the blood of man, by man shall his blood be shed, for God made man in His own image." He draws a connection for us that leads from our human blood to His divine image. Even though sin has corrupted that image to such an extent that it can now only be described as being lost in our fallen human race, it still matters to the Lord so much that He demands a strict accounting for blood for every individual member of His highest creation.

When Moses was sent to unleash the divine plagues against Pharaoh and all Egypt, blood was involved both first and last. The opening salvo was a direct hit on the Nile River. This lifeline of the land of Egypt—which was the only reliable source of water for the entire area—flowed red with blood to make the message clear to Pharaoh that the Lord, the one true God, would come through to rescue His chosen people. When it came to the tenth and final plague, blood was not the scourge, but the sign of grace and favor instead. The blood of the Passover lamb painted on the believers' doorposts spoke to that dreaded angel of death, testifying to the Lord's command not to strike the firstborn son inside. So as the Israelite community would continue its journey into the wilderness, they would constantly be made fully aware of the high importance that God places upon blood.

It should have therefore come as no surprise to anyone witnessing the ceremonies in and around the tabernacle that blood played a central role in these holy activities. The altar was stained red. The floor in front of the tent curtain was spattered. The priests at their ordination were marked by blood quite literally from head to foot. Blood set apart and sealed a testimony that had been sent straight from the mouth of Almighty God. It was with them when they were rescued from slavery, and it remained with them as a sign and guarantee of their salvation and inheritance in the Promised Land.

All of this seems strange to us today because it seems that among us we make every effort to ensure that we see very little blood in day-to-day life. It must be okay to have blood on television, with all of the murder that is depicted in popular crime drama shows. It certainly does get our attention there. But when it enters the realm of reality, blood screams at us, saying that something is very wrong—it makes us extremely uncomfortable. What would be important for us to consider in our situation is to take note of the use of blood in the upcoming liturgical directions that we will study, and to link them directly to Christ. On the one hand, it is the life of Jesus that is presented in sacrifice on the cross in exchange for our life, to the end that total forgiveness is granted us freely through His blood. On the other hand, since blood is also promoted in Holy Scripture as a connection to the image of God, it speaks to a total restoration of that image, a purification that is achieved when our Lord and Savior makes us one in perfect communion with Him by the Holy Spirit.

4 Vestments (Leviticus 8:1–13; compare Exodus 28 and 39; Numbers 15:37–41)

A uniform tells a story about a vocation, even more so than about the individual filling it. This can be said about the mail carrier, soldier, and hotel concierge, but especially so when you're talking about a servant of God's Word. Every detail, down to the colors and accessories, communicates an unmistakable message both to the giver and the receiver of God's gifts. Vestments remind the officeholder that he occupies a sacred position in which his faithfulness is essential to the spiritual health of the people under his charge. They remind the congregant to pay attention to something more important than just the personality and moral example of the individual standing in front of the altar. The holy office is what God has created, and into which He placed the individual to do His work.

As the priests received their sacred vestments at the Lord's command, they were consecrated and set apart in a ceremony witnessed by the entire congregation of Israel. Oil and blood, sacrifices, and holy meals all played their important part, but it was what these servants wore that endured from day to day as the sign of their office. The men wearing the linen, gold, and precious stones would be the ones handling the holy vessels and bringing the people's sacrifices before the Lord in keeping with His plan to welcome forgiven sinners as His precious children. The vision of the white-robed multitude in Revelation attests to the purity of those who are cleansed by a faith in Christ that is often lived out in the midst of persecution at the hands of the world. They were clothed in white not because they happened to occupy a privileged class of believers or because they were being rewarded for their own merits. The priests' sacrificial work, as the congregation's appointed connection to divine favor, would usher God's saints into this blessed multitude gathered before God's judgment throne.

Aaron would be the first man to fill the high priestly role. As the high priest, he was responsible for the iniquity, the burden that required atonement for the entire nation. His position as mediator would be concretely layered on top of his linen garments. On his shoulders would be placed two onyx stones engraved with the names of the twelve tribes of Israel. The twelve stones on his breastpiece would also include those names. He would wear the golden diadem with the phrase "Holy to the Lord" engraved on it; his sons, the other priests, would have simple linen caps. The lots of judgment known as Urim and Thummim would be placed on his heart as he went into the Holy Place before God's presence.

Is there a connection to the vestments worn by Christian clergy today? Perhaps there is some distant relationship that can be found and described in general terms, but the most direct ancestor of today's vestments seems to be the common dress of the Greek and Roman cultures. As wardrobe changed with the introduction (and sometimes invasion) of foreign peoples, the clergy simply kept wearing what they had on already. Besides, it should be kept in mind that vestments do not speak the same story in the New Testament Church as they did under the Old Covenant. Pastors are not mediators to God in the same sense, nor are they ordained to offer sacrifices for the forgiveness of the people. Christ has fulfilled that high priestly role, and through Baptism, He has made every believer a priest under Him. The pastor's vestments designate him in an altogether different, but still extremely important, kind of calling—one of proclaiming the Word, announcing the forgiveness of sins, and handing out the sacraments that Christ has instituted until He comes again at the Last Judgment.

5 Breaking God's Directions (Leviticus 10; Numbers 12; 15)

When you throw a bunch of rules, ceremonies, and statutes at a large group of poor, miserable sinners, you're bound to have them broken, and it would be safe to assume that this will happen sooner rather than later. But that does not keep the Lord from insisting on His righteous laws anyway. The common objection can be heard to this day, "I thought God was supposed to be gracious, accepting, merciful, and loving! But all I see here is a demanding, rule-bound tyrant!" This sort of statement arises out of a fallacy that assumes as true the very thing it is trying to prove. It presupposes our twisted and self-centered forms of acceptance, love, and mercy. It ignores the Lord's gracious and merciful work in providing a rescue from the sin and death into which we as a human race plunged by Adam's free choice. Since we are not by nature pure and holy, we sinful, evil creatures see those qualities as offensive in their Creator. But it truly is also in our best interest for eternal life and salvation that the Lord our God preserve His holiness, so that He can bestow it upon His children.

As the priests and Levites spent their days performing their vocation in holy places, they were the ones charged to be concerned continually about what is holy and what is defiled. Both holiness and uncleanness can be transferred by touching, and God's laws are very clear on the consequences. More on the concepts of holiness, including the status of clean and unclean, will be discussed in detail later on in this study. For the servants standing before the Lord's tent of meeting, following God's liturgical directions were a matter of life and death! They would have no other choice but to keep them or bear with potentially severe consequences, as Aaron's first two sons, Nadab and Abihu, found out.

Recall the characters in Jesus' famous story of the Good Samaritan as recorded in Luke 10:25–37. After the poor victim was attacked and left for dead by the side of the road, two men—one a priest, the other a Levite—came down the same road but nevertheless passed by on the other side. They felt it necessary to keep their distance, evidently in order to preserve their holy state. Ironically, they wanted to remain able to serve the Lord, yet to do so, they refrained from serving Him in helping one in need! This is why Jesus is so adamant about placing ceremonial service in its proper relationship with acts of mercy. The former defers to the latter when it comes to what our Lord, the true Good Samaritan, has done to save us. Yes, it was incumbent on these priests and Levites to keep every last detail of the Divine Service intact. But it is also important to keep our eyes of faith fixed on Jesus, to whom the Divine Service points, and from whom it bestows the Lord's eternal gifts.

Conclusion

The divinely appointed order of the priests play an important part in the worship life of God's Old Testament people as they wander in the wilderness. But even this fact does not give Aaron and his sons the green light to make themselves power-hungry dictators who command the people to obey by virtue of their spiritual position. They are, rather, continually reminded that they serve the people at the pleasure of the Lord, and at all times are subject to His life-giving Word.

Concluding Activities

Speak a closing prayer, make any necessary announcements, and distribute study leaflet 4.

Clean and Unclean

Leviticus 11–15; Numbers 5; 19; Deuteronomy 14; Luke 2

Preparing for the Session

Central Focus

Ancient biblical concepts such as clean and unclean are all but lost on our contemporary culture. Even to well-versed Christians, the distinctions can seem meaningless and arbitrary. This session will clarify what is going on with this incessant process of purification and shed a possibly unexpected light on our life of joyful repentance.

Objectives

That participants, led by the Holy Spirit working through God's Word, will

1. trace the various activities described in relation to the concepts of clean and unclean;
2. follow along as the process of ritual purification is delineated; and
3. discover the ultimate answer for removing the stain of sin through Christ.

Note for the small-group leaders: Lesson notes and other materials you will need begin on page 66.

For the Lecture Leader

Session Plan

Worship

Begin the session with the hymn printed in the study leaflet. Accompaniments are available in denominational hymnals, such as *Lutheran Service Book* or *Lutheran Worship* (refer to hymnal index). (Note: Concordia Publishing House has available *The Concordia Organist.* All the initial worship hymns in the LifeLight courses are included in this resource. It's especially helpful for mission congregations and small parishes. See the list of study resources on page 7.) Follow with this prayer:

Prayer

Heavenly Father, we are unclean due to our debilitating and disfiguring sin. As You provided for healing and cleansing for those who in ancient Israel were ceremonially unclean, so too in our day, cleanse and purify our hearts with Your Holy Gospel to the end so that we may with true and lasting faith enter Your kingdom and stand on Your holy ground. In the name of Jesus we pray. Amen.

Lecture Presentation

1 Animals (Leviticus 11; Deuteronomy 14)

God is not an egomaniac! He is not wrapped up in Himself, nor does He obsess about to what degree He is set apart from His creation. Since His first walk in the Garden of Eden, God has demonstrated to us that He desires to come close to us. Actually, it should be said, He is all about bringing us closer to Him. His presence among His people was found in a particular place, even though one could really say He is present everywhere. There are people who insist that since God created nature and is found in it, in a perfect landscape or sunset, they would rather stay close to Him in that sort of venue. But that kind of thinking is actually an insult to our omnipresent and loving God, whose eager desire is to welcome us into His gracious presence, through which He grants us His forgiveness and precious gifts.

What people don't like about that gracious presence isn't the forgiveness, life, peace, and love of God—at least not anyone I have met would object to those good things. Rather, they are reticent to come to His house because of the demands of His absolute purity and perfection. Perhaps you have heard someone joke that "The roof would fall in if I were to darken the door of my church!" This betrays a certain fear that can be simply described as "God is good; I know I am not, but I don't know how I'm going to get around that problem. I have led a life of which I am not too proud. I feel defiled because I was hurt by someone else's sin. I am angry with another person or with God Himself, and I have no way of putting my attitude in the right alignment with what He asks from His believers and worshipers. I would just as well leave the Lord alone, if only He will be a nice guy and return the favor."

It's possible that the Israelites felt this way too as they wandered in Sinai's wilderness. Of course, God would not leave them alone! He acted in His amazing and miraculous way to pull them out of bondage in Egypt and inch them ever closer to the Promised Land of their ancient inheritance. Among our Lord's greatest desires is to be intimately involved with His people. His perfect presence would mix in and among the people's sinfulness. But until He could do so in human flesh, that is to say, until the fullness of time, when our Lord and Savior Jesus Christ would appear, being born of the Virgin Mary, He would have to come near in a lesser way, through the tabernacle, and later on by means of the temple.

Even though this man-made tent and golden ark of the covenant is inferior to the perfect body of Christ, it is still going to be, for several centuries, the center of God's purity. From this point outward, our Lord makes things holy and welcomes them into His presence. Anything from outside the accepted circle transfers not purity, but the very opposite—uncleanness. God's Word of commandment attaches to His creation and makes distinctions that will help guide His people as they strive to keep His Law and retain His blessing.

How do you know if an animal is clean or unclean? For a land animal, it needs to fulfill two basic requirements to be clean: chew the cud and possess a cloven hoof. Sheep, goats, and oxen are approved—they exhibit both distinctions. Horses, dogs, pigs, and rabbits are unapproved, and so are declared "unclean to you"—they miss one key feature or the other. Seafood needs to have had fins and scales before it is allowed on the plate. Insects need to be hoppers, not crawlers. Reptiles and amphibians are out—God says these living creatures will defile His people. Avoiding the animals that do not make the cut may perhaps have kept the Israelites from the risks of either disease or pagan worship, but that is not the full story about why these Old Testament distinctions were put in place. Even though Jesus removed the requirements behind which animals are approved or not, it is still fruitful to look into what this practice meant for God's ancient people. From our perspective of totally restored freedom, we can find it hard to identify with these requirements of clean and unclean. But as we dig a little deeper, we can get a better insight into the God who desires to draw near to us and clothe us in the garments of His truth and purity.

2 Childbirth (Leviticus 12; Luke 2:22–39)

How can bearing children be unclean? Does this mean that women and the important things that only they can do by God's design are to be considered impure and unworthy of His blessing? Did our Lord give the command to humanity to "be fruitful and multiply" or not? How can a society put a woman through the agony of ritual purification when she cannot help but to go through the natural cycles that happen to her? And why is it that the time necessary for purification is twice as long when a mother gives birth to a daughter?

As you may have already perceived, if there would be anything about the Old Testament's ceremonial laws that will not make sense, it will somehow involve those laws that pertain to this topic. In fact, some very devout and Bible-believing people will throw up their hands in disgust at the very thought of someone declaring a woman unclean after childbirth or a monthly period. This is all understandable, because now we tend to put everything in Scripture into terms of right and wrong, and we view things that are clean and unclean with the same polarity. Although ritual uncleanness does have some relationship to sin and the curse of the fall, it still is not identical with moral transgression. In other words, the Bible is not saying that it is sinful to give birth or undergo menstruation. These are liturgical directions, not value judgments. Neither God nor any primitive or so-called "male-dominant" society is condemning women, or relegating them to any inferior standing, as is sometimes heard today.

To make sense of this section of legislation, it helps if you refer back to what the Scriptures say concerning blood. Whatever the source, whether human or animal, blood is sacred and out of ritual bounds, if you will. Blood is respected, and most of all, the blood of Christ is revered as the source of our life now and forever. Childbirth produces a flow of blood, and even though in this case the biological matters are different, the blood still deserves its ritual respect. The process of ritual purification, whether a woman gives birth to a boy or girl, begins with a period of uncleanness, where all contact is to be avoided. At the end of her time, she offered sacrifices for purification.

These curious regulations play their most significant role in the Christmas story, when in Luke 2, the record attests to Mary and Joseph faithfully fulfilling their ritual duty after Jesus is born. Bethlehem was within a day's walk to the temple in Jerusalem, so they brought the Holy Infant, God the Son in human flesh, before the altar of God the Father, even though, notes Dr. Kleinig, "the law did not require the son (Jesus) to be present for this" (*Leviticus*, p. 270). The Gospel informs us that the offering required to purify Mary's ritual uncleanness was a pair of birds instead of a lamb and a bird, an allowable substitute if one could not afford a lamb. It has been inferred from this that Mary and Joseph were poor, which may be accurate, but it must also be remembered that they had just traveled from Nazareth following a surprise census order, so acquiring a lamb for Mary's purification rite may simply not have been possible for them at that particular time. In a way, you could also explain their action by pointing out that Jesus Himself was the Lamb who would be offered on the cross when the proper time came. At any rate, the lowliest form of ritual purification would receive the highest honor in its fulfillment in connection with the coming of our Savior, who once dwelt in the tabernacle, then in the temple, and finally, in true human flesh. The curse of sin that attached to childbearing, according to Genesis 3, and that every Israelite woman recalled in her vocation, would, through Christ, be eradicated for the purification of the entire human race.

3 Leprosy (Leviticus 13; Numbers 5)

Ah, the classic biblical "unclean" skin disease! Leprosy in all its vivid detail is described for us in Leviticus and Numbers, and instances of it abound throughout the rest of Holy Scripture. When you thank God for all the advances that we have seen in medicine and technology over the past three thousand years, remember to especially thank Him for all the effective ways available today to treat the ailments that are addressed in this week's readings! In Leviticus 13, there are several different skin diseases covered, but the term "leprosy" or "leprous disease" is intended to be the all-encompassing category under which these unclean scaly skin conditions are named.

Leprosy is specifically known to us today as Hansen's Disease, and probably did not exist in Palestine during Bible times. The Hebrew term that is found here and in several other places in the Bible is used in modern Hebrew to mean psoriasis. Whatever it was that infected God's people, it was a phenomenon that testified directly to the fallen character of His good creation. It looked like death was setting in on the skin before the person's actual death (see *Leviticus*, pp. 271–88 if you wish to study in greater detail about the topic of leprosy). It's no wonder that these visible signs of death would be forbidden before the sacred presence of the Author of life.

But not all the skin conditions that were encountered by the priests or the laypeople would automatically make them unclean. That is why the Lord, in Leviticus 13, gives so much detail both to Moses and Aaron in order to guide the priests as they diagnose the particular kind of skin disease that they were observing. Was it something that will clear up in a week, or spread to other parts of the body? Would it kill off the hair and set in deep in the skin? Would it appear on the head? The priests had so much to look for that at times it must have boggled their mind to consider the responsibility that they were given. However, these questions were not provided to them in order to treat the ailment. They appear in Scripture to point out what exactly it is that would try to obstruct the gracious work of God, and to reveal those who were in need of healing by Christ, our Great Physician of body and soul.

When the ten lepers met Jesus, according to Luke 17:11–19, they came face-to-face with the One who long before had instructed Aaron's sons on how to recognize their problem. Now that the Lord was walking among His own people in the flesh, He would simply speak the Word that would heal them. Out of faith, these ten men prayed to Him for mercy, and Jesus responded with a command that would have been in full compliance with the directions in Leviticus. "Show yourselves to the priests," would have meant that the lepers would have had to submit to their expert examination to verify their status as either clean or unclean. The one exception, a man who as a Samaritan would not have been eligible to enter the temple courts whether he had leprosy or not, was the one who returned with a thankful heart to Jesus. He alone received the full divine blessing, "Rise and go your way; your faith has made you well."

4 Cleansing (Leviticus 14)

Now that the unclean skin disease has been declared as such, what is an Israelite to do about it? As Leviticus 14 describes, the believer had to follow a long and detailed process that commenced once his particular medical ailment had healed. While the purification procedure was extensive, it included two main functions, broadly speaking. First, the person had to be separated out from the rest of the Israelite community and cleansed of the leprous disease or whatever else had earned him the status of "unclean." Second, the newly cleansed person would be readmitted back to the Israelite community.

The believer's initial separation was not a simple symbolic gesture. Uncleanness could not come into contact with anything holy, so even the priest who would make the judgment as to whether the person was clean or not must also go with him outside the camp—beyond the borders of the community of God's people. The cleansing ritual in this first stage centered on the individual rather than on his relationship to others.

Two wild, yet ritually clean, birds were used at this point, each with two different fates. One was killed over an earthen vessel that caught its blood; the other bird was dipped into the blood of the first one after that blood had been mixed with water. A cedar stick, scarlet yarn, and a hyssop branch were used as a brush to sprinkle the blood and water mixture over the person whose leprosy had been healed. The individual was then declared clean. The live, blood-stained bird was released in the field, presumably to rejoin its flock, while the Israelite himself took a ritual bath, shaved, and washed his clothes. He would then be ready for the second stage, when he would rejoin the group just like that bird whose life was spared.

Cleansing an individual from leprosy was a big deal. We read from 2 Kings that Naaman, the mighty and powerful commander of the Syrian army, had heard the good news through a captured Israelite servant girl that the Lord's prophet could heal him in Samaria. Though the king of Israel himself refused to believe, Naaman was undeterred in seeking out this miracle-working prophet. It was only until Elisha paid no attention to Naaman's credentials, or to anything else humanly significant, that the foreign general paused and very nearly went home remaining leprous in order to save his pride.

It was the heartfelt advice of Naaman's servants who directed him to the muddy, unimpressive Jordan waters. (2 Kings 5:13) "It is a great word the prophet has spoken to you." Even though that word was hidden in utter simplicity and foolishness, the ordinary-sounding Word of God attaches to the water to yield a truly cleansing flood that would purify every disease and sin. Because of this cleansing, Naaman was also mindful of his newly created faith in the Lord. His conscience, in fact, needed help in order to nurture that faith, since his official duties back at home required him to enter a temple dedicated to what he now regarded as a false god (2 Kings 5:17–19). With this God-given gift of faith, a healed and cleansed leper would be eager to rejoin the faithful in the presence of the merciful and forgiving Lord. (Psalm 84:10) "A day in Your courts is better than a thousand elsewhere. I would rather be a doorkeeper in the house of my God than dwell in the tents of wickedness."

5 Purification and Reincorporation (Leviticus 15; Numbers 19)

Once the individual had reclaimed his status as clean, he was allowed back into the camp. This signaled that the second stage had begun, which was just as important as the first. The Israelite must once again become part of the people of God and the congregation of believers. To be sure, we are not talking about someone losing faith and then getting it back. These are liturgical boundaries that we are navigating. Taking part in the Old Testament Divine Service requires that the worshiper be ceremonially clean and worthy to stand before God's gracious presence in the holy sanctuary. A person did not only think about himself as an individual, but always considered the relationship he had with the community and with the congregation.

Even though the person had healed up from his skin disease, had performed the necessary sacrificial procedure, and had been declared clean by the priest, he was still not yet ready to enter his own tent! Seven more days of an "in-between" state must elapse, and then at last, once the person had washed and shaved again, he was allowed not only inside his living quarters but was also expected to approach the holy altar in front of the tent of meeting and offer sacrifices on the eighth day.

Once the animal is sacrificed, the blood of the guilt offering is dabbed on the right earlobe, thumb, and big toe of the right foot. This is similar to what the priests went through when they were ordained: the blood set aside the ear to hear God's Holy Word, the hand to touch holy things, and the foot to stand on holy ground. After the blood comes oil. This is applied at the very same places on the body where the blood was placed. The leftover oil was poured on the cleansed person's head as an anointing that signaled atonement had been made.

Full purification then meant full inclusion in the civic and liturgical life of Israel. Although less-detailed procedures were handed down for other cases of uncleanness (garments, house infection, bodily discharges), the goal of rejoining God's pure liturgical community remained the same. One who would stubbornly refuse to abide by the Lord's set order was ordered to be cut off from His people, a fate equal to dying while in an unclean state (see Leviticus 7:21; 15:31).

There was also the possibility of abiding by the ceremonial statutes but completely disregarding love and true faith in God. The prophets handed on God's warning concerning people who "honor Me with their lips, while their hearts are far from Me" (Isaiah 29:13). Jesus commented on the Pharisees' careful attention to liturgical commandments; yet at the same time, they were unrepentantly opposed to the Lord's own plan of salvation in Christ, so He compared them to whitewashed tombs (Matthew 23:27). These reprimands do not discount the spiritual worth of the Old Testament ceremonies themselves. Rather, they are meant to ensure that faith is their priority so that the community as a whole retains its place as God's chosen people.

Conclusion

Items or people are pointed out in these liturgical directions as "unclean" because in some way (whether they wanted to or not) they ran the risk of hindering the gracious activity of our Holy Lord's coming among His people and welcoming them into His presence. When they were diligent about avoiding impurity and attending to their own cleansing, then they were drawn closer through faith to the God who loves and saves them. In Christ, we have the best cleansing of all, for His is a purification that doesn't merely wash our body but also brings renewal to us in body and soul, gathering us together with His Holy Church.

Concluding Activities

Speak a closing prayer, make any necessary announcements, and distribute study leaflet 5.

Atonement

Leviticus 16–17; 21; 23; Number 29; Matthew 6; Hebrews; 1 John 2

Preparing for the Session

Central Focus

Atonement lies at the heart of Israelite worship during the wilderness wanderings, just as much as it does for us Christians in the twenty-first century. A final, full, and universal atonement was achieved for us by the Son of God, Jesus Christ, our Lord. As the Book of Hebrews attests, He is the focus of this significant ancient ritual event, as well as that of our Divine Service today.

Objectives

That participants, led by the Holy Spirit working through God's Word, will

1. identify the Old Testament concept of atonement and the ceremonial Day of Atonement;
2. link this important ritual to its fulfillment in the cross of Jesus Christ; and
3. incorporate these emphases into a fuller spiritual practice of repentance and faith.

Note for the small-group leaders: Lesson notes and other materials you will need begin on page 70.

For the Lecture Leader

Session Plan

Worship

Begin the session with the hymn printed in the study leaflet. Accompaniments are available in denominational hymnals, such as *Lutheran Service Book* or *Lutheran Worship* (refer to hymnal index). (Note: Concordia Publishing House has available *The Concordia Organist.* All the initial worship hymns in the LifeLight courses are included in this resource. It's especially helpful for mission congregations and small parishes. See the list of study resources on page 7.) Follow with this prayer:

Prayer

Lord Jesus Christ, our atonement sacrifice and advocate before the Father, we thank You for Your selfless self-offering for our sakes, and we praise You for Your full completion of the salvation task. Assure us of Your presence with us to the very end of the age, and fix our eyes both on Your cross, where our atonement was achieved, and on Your Holy Supper, where we find our atonement handed out for our benefit. Amen.

Lecture Presentation

1 Day of Atonement (Leviticus 16; 23:23–32; Numbers 29:7–11)

The Book of Leviticus, which is structured as a manual on how to conduct the Old Testament liturgy, centers its whole emphasis on this fall festival. All the other sacrifices, rules, and ceremonies lead to and from the divine gift of atonement. When the New Testament, especially the Book of Hebrews, explains the meaning of the sacrifices, atonement is foundational. This act of God liturgically connects all those centuries that lie between the first promise of the woman's Seed in Genesis 3:15 and its fulfillment in Christ's death on the cross. In Leviticus, an interlude on matters of clean and unclean separates the tragedy of Nadab and Abihu from the yearly ceremony that the Lord set forth to memorialize that crisis and, more important, provide His priests a way to avoid a similar fate. The emphasis on cleansing that we studied in Leviticus 11–15 in some ways helped prepare us for the all-important once-a-year cleansing that will be described in chapter 16.

Three animals are involved in the atonement ritual. A bull will be sacrificed as a sin offering for the priests. Two goats will await the fate that will arise from casting lots. One goat is for sacrifice to the Lord; the other is a "scapegoat" (KJV; NIV) designated for Azazel (ESV). The blood of the bull and of the first goat will be set aside to complete the atonement ceremony inside the Most Holy Place. The scapegoat will be sent outside the camp and let go into the wilderness, or, as the Hebrew literally says, to Azazel.

Before that happens, though, the scapegoat must complete a very important task. It must serve as an altar of confession, if you will, a receptacle for every sin that is confessed over its head. Both hands of the high priest transfer the sins of the entire community onto this one substitutionary animal, so that it alone bears every iniquity, every wrongdoing, as it is released into the cruel and rugged desert. If Azazel is meant to stand for Satan or hell, then that is where the goat is sent—along with all the sins that were placed on its head. The goat and the sins along with it are never to return, never to condemn the people with the divine punishment that they had deserved.

Our conception of a scapegoat today would most likely stand for a person who takes the blame that in reality had not belonged to him. It isn't fair that this poor soul would have to suffer for the sake of someone else who gets off scot-free. Yet that is the true beauty of the atonement; indeed, it's the beauty of the Gospel—it isn't fair, thank God! Just think of Barabbas, who was released as Christ was condemned to death. Jesus is portrayed in the Gospel Passion accounts as both the sacrifice and the scapegoat. He gave His life as a sin offering for our sake, plus He was led outside the city gate to a lonely hill called Golgotha. There, He was hoisted up as a curse for us, suspended in the spiritual wilderness that lies between heaven and earth, along with the sins of the world taken up with Him and borne on His sacred head, now wounded. After His death, He descended into hell, that is, He was released from death's grip to take on the real Azazel, so that He would announce there His ultimate Easter triumph over hell and its evil lord. No more substitutes were needed. No more sacrifice would ever be required. God's wrath has been fully propitiated. Because of Christ's atonement for you, your sins are never to return to condemn you; the favor of the Lord shines upon you instead!

2 Place of Atonement (Leviticus 17:1–9)

The ark of the covenant. Few eyes have seen it. Mystery surrounds it. Indiana Jones found it, and now some massive warehouse is holding it. Well, that last one is an interesting figment of a movie writer's imagination! But there is no doubt about it—this wooden box, barely the size of a nightstand, overlaid in pure gold and covered by twin golden cherubim, commands unparalleled respect and intrigue all at once. Bezalel, the master craftsman from the tribe of Judah, finished his masterpiece just in time for it to be covered up forever behind the tabernacle veil and (nearly five hundred years later) behind Solomon's massive temple curtain. Even when the ark was moved about during Israel's wilderness wandering, it was always tightly covered in cloth and entrusted to members of a specific Levite clan, the Kohathites, to carry.

Once the tabernacle and its courtyard were set up with the camps of the tribes situated around it, the ark inhabited the very center of God's promised presence and grace among His chosen people. It also was distinguished as the holiest place. The term "Holy of Holies" is a literal translation of the Hebrew, which may be translated as "Most Holy Place." It is used in Scripture both for the tabernacle tent's central room and for the innermost chamber of Solomon's temple (1 Kings 6). Nothing on earth is closer to the Lord than this place is, because upon the ark is His "mercy seat," the throne of grace that only Jesus Christ Himself surpasses. God's Word of promise and His holy name make the place holy, so it will be treated as such.

One of the most dramatic episodes that would demonstrate this point, in a way reminiscent of the tragedy of Nadab and Abihu, is found in the divine outbreak against Uzzah (2 Samuel 6:5–15; 1 Chronicles 13). The ark was on a cart being pulled by oxen, rather than carried by its poles. The beasts stumbled, and Uzzah reached out his hand to hold the ark steady. It could have been a simple reflex on his part to grab the ark, but the action nevertheless called down the full wrath of God upon the unfortunate soul. He was not authorized, just like that out-of-bounds sacrifice that was offered by Aaron's first two sons, and so the outcome was the same—namely, immediate death. This severe punishment made an impression on King David, so out of holy fear and reverence for the Lord, he treated the ark carefully and in accordance with all of the instructions God had given through Moses over four hundred years before.

Additionally, the Lord would not stand for any imitation or competition against either this ark or the place that is set aside for it. Aaron was already well aware that He frowns upon substitute gods, thanks to the golden-calf incident. Centuries later, after the kingdom split, King Jeroboam of the Northern Kingdom would set up two altars at two different sites. His idols of choice for those competing worship locations? You guessed it—golden calves (1 Kings 12:28–29)!

Coming back to Leviticus 17, we can see clearly that the courtyard of the tabernacle is the only acceptable venue for animal sacrifice. If an Israelite goes out and does his own self-chosen variety of worship, whether the infraction happens inside the camp or out in the wilderness, then he hasn't merely overstepped some nit-picking optional rubric. In fact, the Lord says that the perpetrator is guilty of bloodshed and must be cut off from the rest of the community—not a minor penalty! To be sure, lots of animals lost their lives when it came to Old Testament sacrifices, but if the location of that sacrificial slaughter is not God's chosen and designated place of blessing, and if it's not done in the presence of God's chosen servant the priest, then the blessing transforms into the worst possible curse.

3 Agent of Atonement: High Priest (Leviticus 21)

It was only one man, and only one time a year. The high priest, starting with Aaron himself and continuing through the generations only to his direct descendants, was the only one who was eligible to pass through the overlapping curtain on the Day of Atonement (known today in Judaism as Yom Kippur). He didn't go empty-handed, either. The high priest needed an atoning sacrifice and its corresponding blood placed upon himself and some more blood set aside to be sprinkled on the altar and the ark inside the Most Holy Place. Even though the high priest was already a man holy and set apart from the entire Israelite community, he still needed to have his sins removed so that safe access to God's absolute holiness would be ensured. The plain linen garments that he wore exclusively on this day would speak to his distinctive act of humility on behalf of everyone.

What is the difference between the offering for sin made on this day and the regular sin offering (Leviticus 4–5)? Any other day, the sin offering brought before the altar and the priest was intended to cover sins done "unintentionally" (4:2, 13, 22). But on the Day of Atonement, the special sin offering, combined with the liturgy of the sacrificed goat and scapegoat, was counted as a cleansing "from all your sins" (16:30), "all the iniquities of the people of Israel, and all their transgressions" (16:21). This one day was designed to catch everything, to declare total forgiveness for God's people and bring them back to Himself. As great as the Day of Atonement was for Old Testament believers, it was still a mere shadow pointing to when one sacrifice would be made once for all time.

Even though the Day of Atonement came around but once a year, the priests still had to maintain their intermediary status for the other remaining days. As we already saw, the clean and unclean legislation laid extra strict requirements upon them. The priests could not approach a dead body and make themselves unclean, with the exception of their very closest blood relatives (but not even a wife!). The high priest was even more restricted: he had to refrain from touching anyone's dead body, even that of his own father or mother. Priests' marriages had to be holy, their haircuts had to be holy, and their bodies had to be unblemished, uninjured, and untouched by knife or tattoo ink. These clear boundaries were for the good of the entire people of Israel—they made sure that the leaders of their worship would not be enticed by the rituals of any of the popular religions of the nations surrounding them (*Leviticus*, p. 453).

If these required characteristics were not met, then the Lord's sanctuary would be profaned. Profanity is commonly thought of today as consisting only of "bad words." But in biblical usage and in anthropological studies, profanity is simply the opposite of holiness or sacredness. When the Lord's sanctuary is profaned, then that means a holy thing or place was treated as common. Its holiness is disregarded, and it is treated just the same as anything else. We see this in the Second Commandment: "You shall not misuse the name of the Lord your God." Just as God's holy name cannot be treated as though it were some everyday, throwaway cuss word, so His priests cannot act the same toward His holy items for which they are given responsibility in the Old Testament Divine Service.

A distinctive activity that demonstrated the special role that the priests filled in the Israelite community would have been their eating. These priests had access to food that was set aside exclusively for God as an offering. If they or anyone in their family did anything that removed them from the holy realm, including if one of their daughters married someone not in the priestly tribe of Levi, then they were no longer allowed to partake of that sacred food. As you can see, the priests' unique status that set them apart from the rest of Israel was a full-time concern, and it was on their minds constantly, not just when they happened to do their job before the presence of the Lord.

4 Christ the Atonement (Hebrews 2; 5; 7–10; 1 John 2)

When the risen Lord Jesus appeared to the two disciples who were walking on the road to Emmaus on that first Easter evening, He "interpreted to them in all the Scriptures the things concerning Himself" (Luke 24:27). This, the greatest single-session Bible study in world history, had to have taken a good amount of time, because He couldn't have merely reviewed a scant sampling of "proof texts" and then called it good. Jesus revealed to these future preachers of the Word that the whole Old Testament Scriptures, in every detail, was written about Him. Philip put this idea to work when he spoke with the Ethiopian eunuch in Acts 8, and all he needed to work from was a single reading from Isaiah. He was even able to cover the topic of Baptism, which of course is not a separate doctrine at all but part and parcel of the one Gospel truth.

When we say that the whole Old Testament reveals Jesus to us, we are not limiting ourselves only to those instances where our Lord sets an example for us to follow in our moral life. He is the greater Moses, it is true, but not in order to give us more laws, as Moses did for the Israelites. He instead embodies all that Moses handed down from his holy conversations. When we read a book like Leviticus, with all its rituals and purity laws and animal sacrifices, we link them all to Christ, but we do not do so separately, as if Jesus' coming were to be thought of as thousands of coincidences with what had happened before in Israel's history.

Instead, all the details of the Old Testament work their way through a funnel like an hourglass so that, all together as one bundle, they reveal to us our Lord and Savior. That funnel, that one central truth that bundles together all that the Scriptures speak of the Messiah, is described one way in places like Isaiah 52 and 53, and in another way here in the liturgical directions of Leviticus 16. Christ's substitutionary death as the one atonement for the whole world's sins provides that focus of interpretation for everything else to point to Him. To make the connection clear to the Christians in Rome, Paul even speaks of Christ as a "propitiation" or "atoning sacrifice," using the same word that described the ark of the covenant's mercy seat in the Old Testament (Romans 3:25).

If anyone should make a connection to the Old Testament without going through the funnel of Jesus' atonement, then that person will see the Gospel as clouded and compromised, and an attempt at achieving righteousness by observing the Law will start to butt in. But it is not our observance of the Law that brings us righteousness, but rather that we are declared righteous by God through Christ's own perfect obedience and substitutionary death and resurrection. It is not our performing of certain prescribed rituals that makes us righteous, but rather it is through those means that God conveys to us the perfect, eternal righteousness of Jesus. Whether it's preaching and sacraments in the New Testament, or guilt-, sin-, and grain offerings in the Old, they all in their specific ways proclaim and provide the fruits of the once-for-all atoning sacrifice that Christ made on Calvary's cross.

5 Fasting: Response to Atonement (Leviticus 16:29–34; Matthew 6:16–18)

The high and holy Day of Atonement was not only marked by a goat sent to the wilderness, a blood-spattered ark, and a high priest bathing twice. On that tenth day of the seventh month, beginning at sundown the day before, God's people were also meant to deprive themselves totally of work, food, and drink. This notable liturgical rubric makes the Day of Atonement quite similar to the weekly Sabbath, yet because of how the Jewish calendar is arranged, it can fall on any day of the week in any particular year. Though it is not specifically mentioned, I would suppose that the Lord would have suspended the manna delivery for this particular holiday.

What message is intended to be given by a full day of fasting? Because fasting is noted in other places in the Bible as a response of mourning and sadness, like Mordecai in Esther 4:1–3 and the people of Nineveh in Jonah 3:5–9, the practice is linked to serious and somber recollection of sin during the atonement ritual. And well it should be, because those hunger pangs that inevitably accompany fasting are poignant reminders of the curse of death that sin inaugurated back at the Garden of Eden. In fact, when ashes are applied to the foreheads of the faithful in Christendom on Ash Wednesday at the beginning of the season of Lent, the words of the Lord's curse upon Adam (Genesis 3:19) are repeated: "Remember that you are dust, and to dust you shall return" (see *Lutheran Service Book: Altar Book* [Concordia, 2006], pp. 483–86).

Yet, it would help us in our modern age to understand fasting better if we were to explore its joyful quality and its power over evil, in addition to its mournful and contrite attitude. A phrase in one of the Communion prayers in the Divine Service reveals this carefully balanced spiritual sentiment: "With repentant joy we receive the salvation accomplished for us by the all-availing sacrifice of His body and His blood on the cross" (*LSB*, p. 161). What is "repentant joy"? It sounds like an oxymoron, but it happens to be the perfect approach to fasting.

Yes, fasting is also a joyful thanksgiving on the Day of Atonement. Eighty-four-year-old Anna waited for Jesus in the temple with eager anticipation, "worshiping with fasting and prayer night and day" (Luke 2:37). Fasting is an intrusion into the everyday routine, and so it acts as a constant reminder that the significant gift of our Lord's salvation is being given out today. As Jesus instructed in the Sermon on the Mount, fasting, as long as it is done in secret without the pretense of earning salvation by doing the work, is rewarded straight from the generous hand of our heavenly Father Himself. When our Savior sends a violent mute spirit out of a man's young son, both the father and our Lord's disciples feel powerless; yet He assures them that He gives His power to those who exercise their God-given faith: (Mark 9:29) "This kind cannot be driven out by anything but prayer [and fasting; KJV]." Fasting can take many forms; it does not necessarily have to be a twenty-four-hour-long cessation from all eating and drinking, as laid out in the Old Testament directions on the Day of Atonement. According to God's Word, fasting of any variety, as long as it is completely joined together with confident trust in the work of Christ, is an appropriate exercise to assist in prayer and spiritual preparation, even in this day and age.

Conclusion

Why are there in this part of the Bible so many different rules, ordinances, sacrifices, and ceremonies? In a word: Atonement. Not that those separate activities in any way earned an atoning sacrifice for the people, but rather they are put in place so that the atonement that Christ made would be anticipated, proclaimed, and handed out.

Concluding Activities

Speak a closing prayer, make any necessary announcements, and distribute study leaflet 6.

Holiness

Leviticus 17–22; Numbers 6; Deuteronomy 7; 9; 17–18; 21; 24–25

Preparing for the Session

Central Focus

God's holiness is what sets Him apart from all the false gods and distinguishes Him from the creation that fully depends on Him. Thankfully, however, He chooses not to use His holiness as a weapon to distance us from His mercy, but rather grants the power of His holy name to save us, to establish a close relationship with us, and to answer our prayers.

Objectives

That participants, led by the Holy Spirit working through God's Word, will

1. survey the multiple ways that God's holiness is confessed concretely in the Torah;
2. understand why holiness is an essential attribute for both God and Church; and
3. articulate the prophetic office of Christ, using Moses as a pattern.

Note for the small-group leaders: Lesson notes and other materials you will need begin on page 74.

For the Lecture Leader

Session Plan

Worship

Begin the session with the hymn printed in the study leaflet. Accompaniments are available in denominational hymnals, such as *Lutheran Service Book* or *Lutheran Worship* (refer to hymnal index). (Note: Concordia Publishing House has available *The Concordia Organist*. All the initial worship hymns in the LifeLight courses are included in this resource. It's especially helpful for mission congregations and small parishes. See the list of study resources on page 7.) Follow with this prayer:

Prayer

O righteous God, without whom nothing is holy, deal with us not as our sins deserve but according to Your never-ending mercy. May Your holiness not only convict us of our trespasses but also enrich us with pardon and peace. Grant us Your Holy Spirit, that our bodies may be sanctified to be Your temple and Your holy love fill us with service toward our neighbor, not as though we were mere people-pleasers but so we do good works that are acceptable in Your sight; through Jesus Christ, our Lord, we pray. Amen.

Lecture Presentation

1 Blood (Leviticus 17:10–16; Deuteronomy 7:1–16; 21:1–9)

Anything that is holy belongs to the Lord. The substance that carries life in the veins of all creatures is the exclusive property of the Creator. Eating and touching blood was expressly forbidden to God's people in the Old Testament because it was ceremonially holy. We have already seen in this study that the only blood that would be fit to take away the sins of the world is the blood of Jesus Christ. In the New Testament Church, that is the only blood that will be drunk, following Christ's own command. The Life of Christ enters into our bodies for the forgiveness of our sins and the strengthening of our souls. Until that Sacrament was instituted, however, all blood was to be considered off-limits and set aside out of respect for the One who alone creates life.

Not even the priests were exempt from this, even though they had considerable access to the meat of the sacrifices and other privileges that were denied to the rest of the Israelites. Atonement and its result, the forgiveness of sins, are inseparably linked to the shedding of blood, the giving of life. Hebrews 9:22 summarizes this: "Indeed, under the law almost everything is purified with blood, and without the shedding of blood there is no forgiveness of sins." Blood makes atonement by the substitution of life for life. Atonement not only makes a payment for sin, but it also dedicates a purified person or thing to the Lord's exclusive service. That is why the holy items and the priests as holy men are anointed with blood.

The face of the Lord will be set against the person who eats blood (Leviticus 17:10). When the Lord's face shines on us (Numbers 6:25), it is for our eternal blessing. But when His face is set against the transgressor, His grace is removed. It means the atonement was rejected. Faith is not existent, so sins remain without forgiveness. Often, the Lord uses human instruments to exact the punishment in which He sets His face against the offender. In fact, (Deuteronomy 7:10) "He will not be slack with one who hates Him. He will repay him to his face." The armies of Israel are performing a holy service when they shed the blood of their enemies in their divinely sanctioned battles. On His strict command, they are to devote them to complete destruction, which is to set them aside as holy in a judgment sense—the Lord wants these evildoers all to Himself. Their blood demands an accounting to God. If this duty is ignored and something that was meant to be destroyed is kept to oneself, then the Lord's holiness is breached, and He will take out His righteous anger on His own people, if need be (see Joshua 7).

When human blood is shed without a witness, and a perpetrator cannot be found (Deuteronomy 21:1–9), a substitutionary atonement is still required, because that innocent blood is still crying out loud to God, just as Abel's blood once had done. Where it is impossible to take the life of a killer as a vengeance payment for the life of the victim, the elders of the nearest city break the neck of a heifer that had not been worked, in a field that had not been planted, and they wash hands over it. Their presumed "guilt by proximity" must be atoned as they take the solemn oath, "Our hands did not shed this blood, nor did our eyes see it shed" (Deuteronomy 21:7). At the same time that they purge any guilt of wrongdoing from their midst, they lay their own blood on the line, promising by their solemn covenant to undergo the same fate as the cow that had been killed if any of them were revealed as the real murderer.

Why did the prohibition against eating blood continue into the New Testament era, if Christ had "declared all foods clean" (Mark 7:19), and the shedding of His blood was the fulfillment of all Old Testament ceremonies? The answer is provided to us in the first church meeting, the apostolic Jerusalem Council in Acts 15. Gentile Christians, whose culture and routine already gave them the freedom to eat blood, came together for the first time with former Jews who had dutifully followed God's ceremonies until only recently. Lest offense make a whole generation of Jewish Christians cringe with horror at the practice, the wise decision for at least a little while was to refrain until the new freedom could be enjoyed by all with a clear conscience. It was only an issue of bearing with the sensitivities of the weak for a time, and its necessity slowly faded away.

2 Sexual Purity (Leviticus 18; Deuteronomy 24–25)

As closely as blood was related to the holiness of one's life and its atonement, so marriage and sexual purity among the Israelites was related to the holiness of God's faithfulness to His people, and vice versa. Pagan nations, especially the Canaanite people, used sex in a destructive, demonic way. The Lord would punish them for their perversion. Such things were not to be so among the people of Israel. At one time in human history, given that all people came from Adam's seed by way of Noah's genealogy, there had been no choice but to marry within close family relationships. Cain's wife (Genesis 4:17) must have been his sister, and at this early stage in the history of the world, their children were not in danger of any congenital health problems. From the time of Moses on, however, intermarriage would forever be a thing of the past. As sin took its root and the curse degenerated the genetic code, it eventually became an ill-fated idea for closely related people to reproduce. Today, if the parents' DNA is too similar to each other, it could mean serious illness or even deformity in their children.

Leviticus 18, therefore, delineates the limits for what the Lord calls to "uncover the nakedness," His chosen term for sexual contact that is intended for procreation. Nakedness carries with it the shame that was introduced into the world in the Garden of Eden with the fall into sin. Ever since the Lord provided garments of skins to cover Adam and Eve's nakedness (Genesis 3:21), it has been His will to keep that nakedness covered except for the context of marriage and procreation according to His plan. When nakedness is uncovered in the context of a marriage that the Lord has blessed, then it is a holy union, a faithful response to God's earlier command to "be fruitful and multiply" (Genesis 1:28; 9:1).

This positive, constructive viewpoint of God toward marriage and sexuality is found elsewhere in Scripture, while here in Leviticus, as the Israelites are wandering in the wilderness, Moses is careful to hand down negative pronouncements on the subject. The wolf of demonic sexual practice is about to attack the Lord's precious flock at this stage in the game, so they will be needing protection from this intense temptation to follow what the other nations were doing with and to one another. These commandments are not exclusively ceremonial, which is often suggested as a way to explain away the prohibition against homosexuality in Leviticus 18:22. Man lying with man as he would with a woman, so it is argued, was merely a feature of pagan Canaanite religion. Now that this is not a danger for us like it was for the ancient Israelites, the prohibition is said not to apply. Not so fast. For one thing, Romans 1:26–28 is clear that this behavior is "contrary to nature," not merely a transgression against some obscure worship rubric. Similarly, Leviticus 18:22 labels homosexuality as an "abomination," something against God's created order and deserving of His wrath of judgment. He detests and punishes it Himself. Other merely ceremonial concerns are clearly marked as "unclean," or an act that would "profane" the Lord's name. Whatever the sexual offense, the Lord's retribution is swift and decisive. He says the very land itself will vomit out its people, since these sins are directly contrary to both of the Lord's key promises to Abraham, Isaac, and Israel. Evil sexual practice is an assault not only on personal honor, decency, and everything else protected by the Sixth Commandment, but is also an attack on the Lord's command to "be fruitful and multiply." The land is a gift from the Father's gracious hand to His children in every generation. But if there is faithlessness, especially in this area of His people's holiness, then the promise of land would work against them instead. Sexual purity for His New Testament people is just as important for their faith as it was among those of the Old Testament.

3 Holiness Statutes (Leviticus 19; Numbers 6)

"I am the Lord." Over and over, the Lord repeats this simple identification in Leviticus 19, organizing the chapter as though one is to pray it as a litany: (v. 2) "You shall be holy, for I the Lord Your God am holy." Jesus repeated this in the Sermon on the Mount (Matthew 5:48), "You therefore must be perfect, as your heavenly Father is perfect." This statement is, even to this very day, a precious gift for the believer just as much as it is an impossible requirement. He is the one and only source of holiness, and He is willing to bestow His holiness on His people whom the Holy Spirit has gathered together within His specific order of the Divine Service. To be sure, the form of ceremony for the Divine Service has changed based on whether you're talking about before or after Christ's coming. But the holiness that our Lord bestows on faithful believers is what has remained in common through all generations. What we could never do for ourselves by following the Law, Christ accomplished through His holy life, substitutionary death, and triumphant resurrection.

And this truth often prompts the question among a few curious minds: so if righteousness through the Law is unattainable on the part of sinful mankind, then why follow the Law at all? It is a sad characteristic of human nature that it opposes anything that doesn't serve its own needs. There seems to be a constant need for a self-serving motive to feed the desire of the flesh so that it would comply in anything good. It was pointed out earlier that even our attempts at good works are repulsive on their own in the sight of the Lord. In theory, performing "good for goodness' sake" is thought of as laudable and even desirable, but everyday experience doesn't see this done too often. Even when we think we're having a good day, the sinful human flesh is still unworthy of the kingdom of God. What's the use?

The Law is not given for self-salvation. That was precisely the complaint that Christ our Lord lodged constantly against the hypocritical Pharisees. It wasn't their good works by themselves that were wrong. The Pharisees were in fact the model citizens of their society. The problem was really their false faith: their trust in their own good works, an attempt at righteousness by means of the Law. This misuse of the Law does not thereby make the Law bad. The fact that it shows our sin does not mean that we should avoid it. But to believe and teach that the Law is our only real shot at achieving the Lord's favor, or the means to obtain a confident assurance of salvation—that is a direct insult to all that Jesus did for our sake.

Did Samson get his superhuman strength from his hair? He was a Nazirite from birth. The vows and restrictions that were placed upon him are outlined in Numbers 6. Of course, the hair by itself had no impact on the flexing of Samson's muscles. Yes, it is true—once Samson revealed his secret to Delilah and she promptly cut his hair, then he became weak as any other man (Judges 16). But the real story is that the Nazirite is holy to the Lord; the vows follow as signs of one's faithful commitment. For Samson, the Word of God bound him to the position of judge and made him the one through whom God would set everything right for Israel. The strength came from the Lord and was bestowed upon Samson through his vow, and the vow was signified by his uncut hair. The same is true with all the other laws and restrictions that bound Israel, with or without a special vow.

The laws themselves did not give righteousness. Rather, the gift of faith granted by the Holy Spirit was exhibited in the lives of God's people through the ceremonial statutes. By their very lives, they confessed what He revealed to them: I am the Lord your God.

4 Idolatrous Practices (Leviticus 20; 22; Deuteronomy 9:1–12; 17:1–7)

The Promised Land was filled with many nations of people whom the Lord promised to wipe out before Israel was to arrive there under the leadership of Joshua. Their various religious practices were incompatible with the worship that God had already set up for His holy people through Moses, so these too were to be totally obliterated. He made a distinction of them, declaring them holy among all other people, so they are to distinguish Him as the only true God and recognize His absolute holiness apart from all the other gods that had inhabited the ancient pantheon.

The Israelites were warned beforehand about what they were going to see once they crossed over the Jordan River. They could not risk being seduced by the temptation of worshiping other gods because that kind of infidelity would spell trouble for the heirs of the divine promise. They cannot share time between God's holiness in the Divine Service and the unclean practices that worshiped the false gods whom He already defeated. He insists on Himself as sole provider of every good gift for His people. This is what the Ten Commandments mean when they teach about having a jealous God.

Idolatry did not only sever a believer from God and the Israelite community; it also negatively impacted the family and its relationships that were meant to thrive under His blessing. The love of a husband for his wife and that of parents for their children was in jeopardy, given what these pagan gods demanded in their false religions. Dr. Kleinig writes about one that is mentioned in particular: "Molech was a deity who resided in the underworld. He required child sacrifice as the price for the fertility of a family and the prosperity of its land. Molech may have been associated by the Canaanites with the spirits of their ancestors, the ghosts of the people who formerly lived on that tract of land and were buried there. That land could therefore be held to belong to them spiritually. They had the power to bless or harm those who occupied their territory" (*Leviticus,* p. 433). Incidentally, you wouldn't have to go far even in today's world in order to find someone who would be tempted to believe such things!

If you wanted a large family, plentiful crops, and abundant wealth, then the gods of the land would seduce your devotion to them. Many Israelites would desire these worldly perks, even to the point of sacrificing their own children in fire rather than listening to the pure Word of the Lord, the one true source of blessings both temporal and eternal. When one of God's holy people would break one of these statutes, and thus defile His holy dwelling in their midst, sometimes God Himself would cut them off and render punishments such as infertility—the very scourge they might have been frantic to avoid. Other times, the people were called upon to exclude the offenders, stone them, or even set them on fire. If the entire community were to become engrossed in iniquity, the land of promise itself would spew them out like a stomach ridding itself of poison. But under God's blessing, coupled with the expulsion of the demonic deities and their worship practices, the land would produce not only the essentials of life, but also abundantly over and above man's desire, just as the Lord had promised: milk and honey.

5 The Prophet (Deuteronomy 18:15–22)

John the Baptist was asked, "Are you the Prophet?" to which he answered in the negative. He was instead the one assigned to prepare the way (John 1:19–23). Nevertheless, the question tells us that the expectation for the fulfillment of God's Word through Moses was still in the minds of some believers 1,400 years later. This was the Messiah we were talking about, the Prophet like Moses who would be raised up to proclaim God's Word to all who would hear it. From the Seed of the woman in Genesis 3 to the Suffering Servant of Isaiah 53 to the Son of Man in Daniel 7, Israel knew that the Christ would be set apart for the holy task of the world's salvation. In the fullness of time, the Lord would raise Him up, just as Moses said, because He would be the true Son of God living and walking among us in human flesh.

Moses had a distinction as a prophet that was unique in the entire Old Testament, as Deuteronomy points out in its conclusion: (34:10–12) "There has not arisen a prophet since in Israel like Moses, whom the Lord knew face to face, none like him for all the signs and the wonders that the Lord sent him to do in the land of Egypt, to Pharaoh and to all his servants and to all his land, and for all the mighty power and all the great deeds of terror that Moses did in the sight of all Israel." The promised, future Prophet would be "like Moses," only greater, because instead of knowing God face-to-face, as Moses did, the Messiah would *be* the face, the very image of God. He would not exhibit mere "signs and wonders" toward men, but He would be sent to do battle with Satan Himself and defeat the ancient serpent and the whole host of hell.

The Prophet Messiah would not, however, unleash the direct glory of God in a fearful fury or achieve a political victory for the oppressed nation of Israel. His would be a spiritual power instead, hidden in weakness and centered in suffering and the cross. His prophetic Word would teach all nations, because His Holy Word would be accompanied by the Holy Spirit, working faith in all those who are baptized in the triune name.

In order to verify that any prophet after Moses, including Christ, the great Prophet, was in fact sent from God, the Lord provided Israel a test to apply to that particular prophet's words. That prophet must speak in the Lord's name, and not in the name of any other god. If what that prophet speaks in the name of the Lord does not come true, or is not in line with the Word that the Lord has already revealed, then the people need not fear him as God's servant. The Lord will not let a fraud prevail in His appointed office of prophet. If those so-called experts would have simply applied this test to Jesus' claims, they might have had the chance to see that Moses, in fact, had predicted His coming and maybe they would even have believed in Him. But as it was, they followed their own works-righteous criteria, and so themselves fulfilled Scripture when they put Him to death on the cross. Whenever Jesus speaks as the Prophet, even among us in the Divine Service today, He does not set forth new commandments as a second Moses, but rather, He proclaims the Gospel of salvation and adoption of all believers into His holy kingdom.

Conclusion

Someone or something that is holy is the Lord's possession. Israel was "baptized into Moses" at the Red Sea (1 Corinthians 10:2); we Christians were baptized in the name of Father, Son, and Holy Spirit. In both cases, a holy people were set aside for faith in Christ for the forgiveness of sins. This forgiveness, paid for by the holy blood of Jesus, brings with it a new life of the believer who is constantly getting acquainted with his or her new identity as a holy child of God. The Word of Christ, who is the Holy Prophet like Moses, strengthens and preserves that holiness until the believer reaches a blessed end.

Concluding Activities

Speak a closing prayer, make any necessary announcements, and distribute study leaflet 7.

Festivals

Leviticus 23–25; Deuteronomy 15–16

Preparing for the Session

Central Focus

The idea of having a Church Year originally came from God. Israel was commanded to observe days and seasons in their ceremonial law so that the Lord's mighty works of salvation would be declared in its fullness. Though today we are free from these commandments, we would do well to continue commemorating the boundless mercy of our heavenly Father that has been revealed to us in His Son.

Objectives

That participants, led by the Holy Spirit working through God's Word, will

1. gain a better grasp of the main holidays and observances covered in these books;
2. compare these holy days with celebrations within the Christian tradition; and
3. grow in their own spiritual preparation as it is conditioned by the Church Year.

Note for the small-group leaders: Lesson notes and other materials you will need begin on page 77.

For the Lecture Leader

Session Plan

Worship

Begin the session with the hymn printed in the study leaflet. Accompaniments are available in denominational hymnals, such as *Lutheran Service Book* or *Lutheran Worship* (refer to hymnal index). (Note: Concordia Publishing House has available *The Concordia Organist*. All the initial worship hymns in the LifeLight courses are included in this resource. It's especially helpful for mission congregations and small parishes. See the list of study resources on page 7.) Follow with this prayer:

Prayer

O blessed, Holy Trinity, Your Church celebrates Your mighty acts of salvation throughout the year. Although our seasons and celebrations have changed over time, continue to kindle in us a strong faith that is not titillated by quickly passing fashion but longs to be fed with the sincere milk of the Word. Lead us to see Christ in every festival of Israel and also now as our teacher, host, and food in the Divine Services of which we are privileged to partake in our time. In Jesus' name we pray this. Amen.

Lecture Presentation

1 Sabbath (Leviticus 23:1–3; 25:1–7; Deuteronomy 15)

The word *holiday* is formed from the words "holy day." The Sabbath was the first day in creation's history set aside as holy, so the Sabbath is the first holiday. It leads the list of feasts that are set aside as holy in Leviticus 23. The Sabbath Day is the holiday that occurs the most frequently in the year. The Lord who never faints nor grows weary set aside a weekly day of rest, which He specifically observed Himself on its inauguration. Was that the only time? We are not told in Scripture whether our tireless God ever rested again whenever the Sabbath Day came around. It probably doesn't matter, for as Jesus Himself said, (Mark 2:27) "The Sabbath was made for man, not man for the Sabbath." This first of all holidays was a gift, a sign of grace from our Creator, a window that is opened each week for God's people to receive good things from His generous hand.

As with all the feasts, the Sabbath is a group event, not a one-on-one spiritual arrangement. "Holy convocations" are gatherings initiated, defined, and carried out by the Lord Himself for those who believe in Him to participate together as one. People meet together at God's command, but they especially are given the promise that He will be there to meet with them. When Jesus promises, (Matthew 18:20) "Where two or three are gathered together in My name, there am I among them," He ties the whole history of Old Testament worship into Himself. The other festivals flow from the Sabbath and, in their own unique way, are reminiscent of its anticipation of God's dwelling with man on earth.

Shabbat meant "to cease," and when an Israelite simply stopped and set aside his work on the seventh day of the week, he was fully participating in the Sabbath ritual. Having worked for six days, he looked forward to the rest that God had promised him. Psalm 95 speaks of the time when the Lord denied His ultimate Sabbath rest to those who had rejected Him: (v. 11) "Therefore I swore in My wrath, 'They shall not enter My rest.'" The Epistle to the Hebrews discusses this verse at length, and there it gleans from the Psalm a rich Gospel treasure, the promise of divine rest. Here is what God's Word proclaims: (4:9–10) "So then, there remains a Sabbath rest for the people of God, for whoever has entered God's rest has also rested from his works as God did from His."

Christ Himself gives the gift of rest to us, because we could not have worked for it by ourselves. He says, (Matthew 11:28) "Come to Me, all who labor and are heavy laden, and I will give you rest." This release from the curse, that is, the thorns and thistles of toilsome labor, is the perfect fulfillment of the Sabbath Day, and part of the reason why Jesus during His ministry performed so many healing miracles on the Sabbath. He wasn't doing it merely to pick a fight with the authorities and make it seem like this was the only way He could think of in order to get Himself crucified. He came to demonstrate His lordship over the Sabbath, as the chief gift-giver on a day that was set aside to receive such gifts.

The Sabbath came on the seventh day to round out Creation and set the repeating pattern for the days of the week. The number 7 is the Bible's most consistent number of completeness. Full peace and complete blessing that is sent to the believer straight from the loving face of our heavenly Father is described among the Hebrew-speakers as *shalom*. On the Sabbath Day, that shalom gift is acknowledged, and the Lord is praised for His provident abundance that had been showered upon His people up to that point.

There is even a Sabbath year, in which God's people, as an act of faith, rely upon the yield of the fields and vineyards of the Promised Land for the previous six years in order to feed them for the entire seventh year. Not only does this year of rest serve to rejuvenate the ground and the vine, but it also reminds the Israelites of their Lord's unending loving kindness. This statute of the Sabbath year is so important in the eyes of God that when the people centuries later are defeated and many of them are exiled to Babylon, the inspired authors make a point of saying that the time of separation, sad as it may have been in the history of Israel and Judah, nevertheless constituted a necessary period of rest in order for the land to observe its missed Sabbaths, as had been predicted already by Moses (Leviticus 26:34; fulfilled in 2 Chronicles 36:21).

2 Passover (Leviticus 23:4–8; Deuteronomy 16:1–8)

The Lord's pivotal act of salvation for His people in the Old Testament was the exodus. Moses' legislation of preparation for the tenth and final plague became for Israel the yearly feast of Passover. This festival is distinguished from the others on the calendar in several ways, but you certainly ought not forget that it is meant to take place at night. The other feasts that are found on the Hebrew liturgical calendar are not as specifically tied to the evening hours as is the Passover. It recalls the patient vigil waiting for the Destroyer's midnight pounce on the Egyptian enemies, while at the same time, the Israelites were hastening their meal, about to make the famous escape under the cover of darkness with nearly two million of their closest relatives. The feast and the salvation event were inseparable, because they were two sides of the same coin. Every Passover participates in God's mighty work, no matter how many years and miles have passed since that first night. When Israel's families eat that unique meal, they are involved in an act of faith that lands them back squarely in that moment in history when the Lord called them out of bondage and initiated them into the reception of His grace.

While the exit from Egypt itself was accomplished in one night, the Passover festival remembrance extended over seven days. This is called the Feast of Unleavened Bread, in which God strictly warned the people through Moses not to eat or prepare any other kind of bread during this special week. To mark His people as holy and pure, He did not even want any yeast to be found in the house. The seventh day following the sacrifice of the Passover lamb (or *Paschal* lamb) is observed as though it was a Sabbath—no work is to be done. The regular Sabbath Day that falls somewhere between the beginning and end of the Feast of Unleavened Bread is considered to be a high day (John 19:31), and the day before it would also be a significant day of Preparation (Mark 15:42).

Just as the Passover was a constant marker on Israel's calendar and reminder of God's hand in the nation's history, so also the festival provided the Gospel writers with noteworthy markers of Jesus' life and ministry.

The boy Jesus was amazing the Jewish teachers in Jerusalem's temple during the Passover (Luke 2:41). John especially makes a point to include references to Jewish festivals as they dot the progression of our Lord's journey to the cross in Jerusalem. In his Gospel, John tells us that Jesus cleansed the temple on a Passover visit (2:13–17), fed the five thousand and walked on water while the feast was "at hand" (6:4), and raised Lazarus just prior to the particular Passover observance during which He would be the Lamb of sacrifice (12:1).

And when that final Passover arrived, Jesus celebrated it with His own disciples in the famous upper room; then He instituted the Holy Supper that would replace the Passover and bring it to completion. The unleavened bread was no longer going to point to the exodus, but rather to the cross. The "cup after supper" would be shared among those reclining at the table, so that everyone together participated in the blood of Jesus for their salvation. Whereas the Passover gave the Israelites an opportunity to "be there" with their ancestors as they walked out of Egypt, the Lord's Supper gave to the disciples (and gives to us Christians) the participation in Christ's once-for-all sacrifice for their sins. We don't have to imagine ourselves standing on the hill of Golgotha long ago and far away. The Sacrament of the Altar, no longer a once-a-year event, but now a continuous, ongoing festival of the Church, has brought the fruits of the tree that is the cross, and places pure forgiveness on our lips.

3 Firstfruits and Weeks (Leviticus 23:9–22; Deuteronomy 16:9–12)

The first barley harvest of the new growing season would have been gathered in at the same time as the Passover (of course, not on the days when they were to rest from all work). But before anyone in Israel would be allowed to eat from the fruits of their labor, a sheaf of barley had to be offered to the Lord first—that's why it is called the *first*fruits. Notice that when the grain is waved in front of the Holy Place, the result is "so that *you* may be accepted" (Leviticus 23:11; emphasis added). The point of presenting the firstfruits is not so that God will approve of our gifts to Him, but rather that He looks upon the faith that He Himself has planted in the hearts of His faithful people.

Israel may have come to the Promised Land and purged it of all other nations, but they must always keep in mind that the land is the Lord's and their crops that they produce through blood, sweat, and tears are nevertheless their provision from the heavenly Father.

The manna supply may have ceased once they crossed the Jordan, but God still gave them bread—only now it is through the means of their own work. The priest is the one who waves the first sheaf on behalf of all the people, together with a lamb, an incensed grain offering, and a drink offering of wine. He marks the time when the people would be free to partake of the harvest, not only in the sacred space but also at home.

From this day onward, a block of seven weeks is counted off in order to make it a perfect "week of weeks." The harvest was designated to take place during these forty-nine days. The conclusion of the harvest would be a special feast on the fiftieth day, later known by the Greek word for the number fifty: *Pentecost*. At this time, leavened bread was offered up, along with several offerings of lambs, rams, bulls, and goats. Whatever was not a burnt offering was intended as holy food for the priests to eat. The Early Christian Church kept that Pentecost tradition going for at least a century or two, presenting offerings of food that would give provision for their pastors (*Didache* 13, referenced in Kleinig, *Leviticus*, p. 509).

Not all the grain was to be picked up when it was harvested in Old Testament-era Israel. The reapers had to leave some grain standing by the edge of their field and not pick up any stalks that lay on the ground. By the Lord's own decree (and everything belongs to Him, anyway) *that* grain belonged not to the farmer but to the travelers and the poor who had nothing to harvest of their own. You could say that the grain along the walking path was left sitting there waiting for the time when Jesus and His disciples would walk past and pick some heads of grain to eat for their journey (Matthew 12:1–8)!

The Feast of Weeks receives its fulfillment in Christ, whom Paul calls the firstfruits (1 Corinthians 15:20, 23). This is because He rose from the dead on the same day that the barley sheaf would have been presented, and that first day of the new week would indicate for Christians a new kind of holy day, one not quite like the Sabbath was for ancient Israel. The day of our Lord's resurrection from the dead would, from the very beginning, be commemorated in the Church every Sunday, but it would be especially observed on the Sunday nearest the time when the Paschal lamb would have been sacrificed. This is why an overwhelming number of languages to this day use some form of "Pascha" for this holiday. The name "Easter" doesn't come up until later on in Church history, when the Gospel finally moves north into Germany and England.

The Feast of Pentecost has also been fulfilled and transformed, as Acts 2 so clearly describes. On this "birthday of the Church," the Old Testament ritual dedication of the end of the grain harvest has become the Holy Spirit's inauguration of a spiritual harvest of souls that will not come to an end until Christ comes again in glory. So the season of Pentecost in the Christian Church Year, the longest one on the calendar, traces the time of the Church in its sacred duty of preaching the Gospel to all nations until, at the end of the season, the faithful turn their attention to the Last Judgment and life everlasting.

4 Trumpets, Atonement, and Booths (Leviticus 23:33–44; Deuteronomy 16:13–17)

The seventh month of the Israelite religious calendar was considered a Sabbath month, situated as it was in the season of autumn opposite the spring/early summer observances of Passover and Pentecost. On the first day of this month, the festivities would begin with the blowing of trumpets, as if a herald were announcing the commencement of the month and calling attention to what would follow as the month progressed. The Lord, the King (Psalm 98) is about to come among His people to perform His gracious act of atonement. Two kinds of trumpets are mentioned in Old Testament religious festivals: a hollowed-out ram's horn and a pair of silver bugles. There is biblical evidence that both were blown at the beginning of each month of the year, at the new moon (Numbers 10:1–10; Psalm 81). But as the seventh month begins, the new-moon trumpet blast begins a countdown to the tenth day, that is, the all-important Day of Atonement, which we have already studied.

Following this day of rest, sacrifice, and fasting that is given in response to the atonement ritual, the Festival of Booths commences on the fifteenth day of the seventh month. It is meant to be a seven-day-long observance for all Israel to gather together and offer their sacrifices. The first day of the feast is marked by solemn rest, gathering in the fruits of the land, collecting branches, palms, and willows, and rejoicing before the Lord at His Holy Place, an observance that is to last for seven days. For those seven days, the Israelites are to dwell in temporary shelters called booths or tabernacles, and these are erected near the Presence of the Lord. The eighth and final day is a kind of "closing ceremony," in which another solemn day of rest is commanded.

The Feast of Booths is a commemoration of the wanderings of God's people in the wilderness. It serves as a reminder to them, even when they have finally reached the Promised Land, that they had to depend entirely upon the Lord and be content with their temporary dwellings. The booths also put them in mind of the tabernacle that God had designed as His chosen place to meet with His itinerant people for their blessing and the acceptance of their offerings. It can remind believers of every time and place that we have a temporary dwelling here on earth. As God's Holy Church, we are set apart from the world in which we live only for a short time, but our true home is with the Lord in His eternal, heavenly presence.

The close proximity of Booths and the Day of Atonement on Israel's calendar helps explain how these observances are related. This is a time of pilgrimage for all of God's faithful to gather and rejoice in the presence of the Lord, who has accepted the blood of atonement for the forgiveness of their sins. The temporary tents are meant to remind future generations so that they "may know that I made the people of Israel dwell in booths when I brought them out of the land of Egypt: I am the Lord your God" (Leviticus 23:43). Just as the Passover was tied to the beginning of the exodus event, so the Festival of Booths commemorates its result. Both of these, in their spiritual message, as well as in their place on the Hebrew festival calendar, center around the Day of Atonement, which is itself an act of rescue that points forward to Christ crucified—our God who "tabernacled" (ESV: "dwelt") among us (John 1:14) in human flesh.

5 Jubilee (Leviticus 25:8–55)

Every day, hundreds of people drive past Independence Hall in Philadelphia; most are likely oblivious to the presence of the Liberty Bell inside. There are words of Holy Scripture engraved on that bell, citing in King James elegance: "Proclaim Liberty throughout all the Land unto all the inhabitants thereof." Quite the theological statement, that is, to claim to find in the forming of the American republic a permanent fulfillment of God's gift of the jubilee that is described in Leviticus 25.

Freedom, release from slavery, a divine inheritance of land—that is all part of Israel's story in these wilderness wanderings. As with all the other festivals, the jubilee reminds God's people that they were bought and ransomed by their Lord. They and their land are not their own; He has lent them everything they have so that they can serve Him as His stewards. As we already have seen, every seventh year is a Sabbath year, a whole year in which all sowing or reaping is put on hold to give the land a rest. Every seventh round of Sabbath years is followed by a jubilee, that is, a holy fiftieth year. During that year, any land that was sold is to be released back to the original owner, the one who first received the land as a gift from the Lord. Anyone who, out of poverty, sold themselves as a servant would be granted release when the jubilee arrived, and that Israelite would return to his rightful property to start all over.

Those who commissioned and designed the Liberty Bell had a healthy patriotic optimism for the young United States of America. They also had a detailed knowledge of the Bible, even if the verse wasn't exactly quoted in its proper context. The true freedom that was foreshadowed by the proclamation of the jubilee in Leviticus would not find completion in any temporal nation; rather, this freedom is found only in Christ our Lord. (John 8:31–32) "If you abide in My word, you are truly My disciples, and you will know the truth, and the truth will set you free." Our jubilee comes not in the restoration of land, nor in the earthly blessings of personal rights. Instead, we are released from bondage to sin and restored to our baptismal inheritance, the heavenly "place" our Lord promises to prepare for us (John 14:2). That will truly be an unending festival without equal!

Conclusion

The Lord had His holy people construct a tabernacle in order to mark off holy space in the midst of their campground. In much the same way, He gave directions for them to delineate holy times, chief among them the Sabbath Day every week and seven special holidays that Israel observed every year. Our Christian Church Year has clear ties with this divinely mandated calendar, but we observe its seasons not in obedience to any command, but in joyful proclamation of the Gospel of our salvation, in selfless unity with believers of prior eras and other cultures, and in a conscientious desire to pass along the pure and entire truths of our Lord as doctrine that is fleshed out in practice.

Concluding Activities

Speak a closing prayer, make any necessary announcements, and distribute study leaflet 8.

By the "Numbers"

Numbers 1–2; 16–17; 20–26; 31; Deuteronomy 31; 34; 2 Kings 18

Preparing for the Session

Central Focus

Having already consulted various parts of the Book of Numbers, we will now delve into material exclusive to this book. These events signal a crucial turn in the wilderness wanderings, and will set the stage for what will continue after the Pentateuch comes to a close. Numbers is a book that you definitely do not want to skip!

Objectives

That participants, led by the Holy Spirit working through God's Word, will

1. recognize census and numerology in their contexts as they relate to proclamation;
2. be able to sort through the timeline of events that comprise the wilderness wanderings; and
3. be more comfortable with using material from these books in personal study.

Note for the small-group leaders: Lesson notes and other materials you will need begin on page 81.

For the Lecture Leader

Session Plan

Worship

Begin the session with the hymn printed in the study leaflet. Accompaniments are available in denominational hymnals, such as *Lutheran Service Book* or *Lutheran Worship* (refer to hymnal index). (Note: Concordia Publishing House has available *The Concordia Organist.* All the initial worship hymns in the LifeLight courses are included in this resource. It's especially helpful for mission congregations and small parishes. See the list of study resources on page 7.) Follow with this prayer:

Prayer

Blessed Lord, You brought Your people Israel up to the very last years of their wilderness wandering by a mighty and outstretched arm. Break and hinder, we pray, every evil counsel and will of the devil, the world, and our sinful nature, those enemies who oppose us in our spiritual walk under the shelter of Your salvation. Grant us Your steadfast protection, that we may ever give thanks to You, for Your love and mercy truly endure forever. Amen.

Lecture Presentation

1 Census Figures and Numerology (Numbers 1–2; 26)

The "numbers" in the Book of Numbers refer to two of three censuses that were taken during the forty years that Israel wandered in the wilderness. Joseph had long ago invited his father and brothers to come down to Egypt to live with him, and when they did, they comprised an extended family of only seventy members (Genesis 46:27). Now, at the time of the wilderness wanderings a few centuries later, they were their own nation of around two million people.

The book's first census was initiated at God's command to Moses in the second year after Israel left Egypt. The twelve tribes fall into a particular order, with Reuben's descendants taking the lead, as he was Jacob's firstborn. As in other times where large-scale counting is documented in the Bible, the general rule was that only the men twenty years old and upward were to be counted. The reason provided for this in Numbers 1 is that these are the men "able to go to war" (v. 3), so we gain a little more insight into the purpose of this particular census, as opposed to the previous one (Exodus 30), in which atonement money was collected for use in worship. There is no indication given in Numbers that there were any men either counted or excluded if they were over twenty and yet unable physically to go to war. The tribe of Levi, made up of both priests and assistants, was treated exceptionally because their males were forbidden to fight in battle. Instead, their sole vocation was to care for and guard the tabernacle and other holy areas.

That is why they are counted in Numbers 3, but instead of listing the fighting men, it lists 22,000 males a month old and upward as set aside for holy service to the Lord. They also are designated to stand in as representatives of every firstborn Israelite male born since the exodus, recalling the Lord's words spoken back in Egypt, (Exodus 13:2) "Whatever is the first to open the womb among the people of Israel, both of man and of beast, is Mine." Now that this census was taken, God consecrated all the Levite males in place of all the Israelites' firstborn. With Levi set aside and Joseph split into two tribes named after his sons, Ephraim and Manasseh (fulfilling Jacob's blessing in Genesis 48:5), we still arrive at twelve tribes that are to be counted among the fighting men of Israel.

It is here that we begin to notice the number symbolism that has been woven in and out of the fabric of raw statistics. The amounts of people are not themselves symbolic, as certain critics claim in order to support their doubt that the people of Israel could have amounted to such a huge mass camping and moving about in the wilderness. The symbols are instead found in how the people are grouped. We have twelve tribes, taking great care to keep that number at 12, whether or not Levi is included. There are four groups of three tribal camps, each situated at the four sides of the sacred tabernacle area. We have already seen instances of 7s, 6s, and 50s when we examined Israel's festival calendar.

Numbers have special significance in Holy Scripture. Jacob inherited the Lord's promise that was passed down from Abraham to Isaac. Jacob's twelve sons and their descendants would possess this blessing, and along with it, the promise of the coming Savior. Twelve is the product of 3 and 4, so that the triune God is acknowledged as the one who created and redeemed everything from the four winds, or directions. Jesus preserved the significance of the number 12 for the New Testament Church when He selected that number of disciples who would later be commissioned as apostles. The Book of Revelation contains the ultimate in biblical symbolic numerology.

By the time we reach the final census in Numbers 26, we find ourselves with a new generation of Israelites, the very ones whom their doubting parents had said would be vulnerable to attack if they were to obey God's Word and enter the Promised Land. That whole generation (except for Joshua and Caleb) would die out in the wilderness because their lack of confidence in the Lord disqualified them to see His mighty hand in action for them anymore. Again, the census number would include only the males twenty years old and upward, but instead of listing them as fighting men, the explicit purpose of this head count would be to determine the land that they would inherit (26:53) once the Lord had finished routing their enemies. God demonstrates confidence in His own abilities to follow through on His promises, and that same confidence would be exhibited in those counted in this new census that was taken as they stood on the doorstep of Canaan.

2 Korah and Aaron's Staff (Numbers 16–17)

Conflict was inevitable among this group of sinful human beings who had been given special privileges with respect to the Lord's blessings. By Moses' own admission, he was no greater than any other person among his kindred. In fact, when he was trying unsuccessfully to talk God out of sending him to lead the exodus, Moses insisted that somebody else would be a better fit for the job (Exodus 4:10–13). Now that the Lord had proven His Word true in using Moses as His instrument to perform His mighty works, some of the Israelites would dare to challenge the authority of God's chosen servant. They sinfully perceived a great potential of power and personal gain to be had for themselves if Moses were knocked down a few pegs and they took over the reins.

Some time earlier, this scenario had already played out with Moses' own sister, Miriam. She and Aaron spoke up against Moses, questioning the Lord's exclusive use of their brother's mouth to speak His Word. How could he, the baby of the family and a mere sinner like the rest of us, presume to occupy such a privileged position? But one would think that once the Lord intervened and struck Miriam with leprosy, the message would get across that God knew what He was doing.

This time, in Numbers 16, Aaron would be included with Moses as the target of rebellion. Now that there was a priesthood set apart from God's chosen people, and even made distinct from their own tribe the Levites, another uprising would boil over, this time involving 250 antagonists. The man at the forefront was a Levite named Korah, and he objected that Moses and Aaron placed themselves in exalted positions over against all the other people of Israel. He claimed that everyone among the twelve tribes was holy and had an equal right to approach God's holy presence on their own merits. This is an even more serious indictment than Miriam's was, because she at least acknowledged that the Lord dealt with His people through particular chosen servants. Korah, on the other hand, wanted to trash the entire system that Almighty God had just set forth for His people on Mount Sinai. If it had been successful, Korah's rebellion would have dwarfed the offense of the golden calf.

At this moment of crisis, when the divine Means of Grace itself was threatened, Moses acted decisively, using the same restraint as he did with his own sister, and turned the matter over to the Lord for His judgment. He was confident of his God-given role, yet at the same time, he demonstrated meekness as he prayed for those who attacked him and faithlessly grumbled against the Lord. Aaron responded in like fashion, risking his very life in an attempt to rescue the same people who had utterly disrespected him and his office. In this way, these consecrated servants emulated Christ, who would pray for forgiveness for His enemies, even while they were in the act of putting Him to death. The same pattern would continue into the history of the Christian Church, where we witness Stephen pleading for those stoning him.

God chooses His servants to proclaim His Word and distribute His precious gifts of forgiveness, life, and salvation, not to play favorites, and certainly not to give men an opportunity to exalt themselves. In order to confirm His call of Moses to his position, and that of Aaron to the high priesthood, the Lord performed the miracle that caused the staff of Aaron to bud and bear fruit, as though it were a live tree branch. This staff would remain before the Lord in the ark of the covenant as a sign to God's people that the ones ministering are the ones He chooses according to His perfect order, even if the men themselves occasionally suffer from weaknesses and sins.

Peter, an apostle who often had to learn things the hard way, instructed those who have been placed into the New Testament pastoral office with these words: (1 Peter 5:2–3) "Shepherd the flock of God that is among you, exercising oversight, not under compulsion, but willingly, as God would have you; not for shameful gain, but eagerly; not domineering over those in your charge, but being examples to the flock." In this way, the Lord's chosen ministers will follow the pattern of Christ, who, according to the hymn found in Paul's letter to the Philippians (2:6–8), counted His ultimate authority and equality with God not "a thing to be grasped, but . . . humbled Himself by becoming obedient to the point of death, even death on a cross."

3 Moses Denied Entry (Numbers 20; 27; Deuteronomy 31; 34)

The God of Israel came to Moses' defense when his leadership and prophetic office were challenged by others, but the Lord also held His servant accountable to be completely faithful to the Word of God. His big sister Miriam had just died, along with the generation of people who were forbidden to enter the Promised Land. Moses led the new generation that was preparing to enter, and it was *déjà vu* all over again for him when the massive congregation arrives at Kadesh, near the border of Edom. Just like what happened just under forty years before at Rephidim, which was probably farther south in the Sinai Peninsula (Exodus 17), the people grumbled because there was no water for them in the wilderness. As their parents did before them, this new generation questioned Moses, "Why have you made us come up out of Egypt?" The difference was, they were all born in the wilderness or had embarked on the exodus at a very young age—these people had never seen what Egypt was like!

For Moses, this was all too similar. These people are not going to be reliant on the Lord no matter what He does. Even with the miraculous manna still stuck in their teeth, they long for the mere idea of Egyptian meat and produce instead. The Lord had commanded thirty-eight years ago to strike the rock with the staff as He Himself stood there (Exodus 17:6), but here at Kadesh, Moses was directed only to hold the staff and speak to the rock. This would demonstrate to this new generation of God's people that the Lord's Word alone is sufficient to work His wonders for their benefit.

You can tell just from his words that meek and mild-mannered Moses had just about had enough! (Numbers 20:10) "Hear now, you rebels: shall we bring water for you out of this rock?" And in that one act of open defiance of God's Word, Moses struck the rock not once, but twice to make it plain to everyone watching that it wasn't an accident. The people got their gushing water to stop all their complaining, but the Lord was not pleased. Moses would not get the privilege of leading the people to their promised inheritance, even after all that he went through for them!

We wonder today sometimes at the harshness of this verdict, but it is written to remind us of the Lord's holy jealousy that He teaches us in the Ten Commandments. He punishes the children for the sin of the fathers to the third and fourth generation of those who hate Him, but shows mercy to a thousand generations of those who love Him and keep His commandments. His desire from everyone is for them to love and trust in Him alone as their God. The Law holds all people in the grasp of its condemnation. In other places of Scripture, Moses stands for the Law and its inability to grant salvation to the souls that it convicts (Romans 8:3). In this, God's mighty leader points to Christ in another way—we need a Joshua, a Savior who by His death and resurrection will lead us forth into the promised land of eternal life. Moses and the Law may grant a glimpse of this from afar, but the Gospel of our Lord Jesus Christ is what grants us forgiveness, life, and unlimited access to the rivers of living water.

4 Bronze Serpent (Numbers 21; 2 Kings 18:1–8)

"As Moses lifted up the serpent in the wilderness, so must the Son of Man be lifted up"; so writes John (3:14) as He records the teaching that Jesus gave to Nicodemus one night. Context suggests that this meeting might have happened at or soon after the Passover festival. The lamb sacrificed for the people nearby at the temple was a witness to faithful Israelites that Jesus had to die in our place. Likewise, Moses' serpent informed catechized believers that our Lord of glory would be raised up on a tree as a curse for us.

At the Chapel of St. Timothy and St. Titus at Concordia Seminary in St. Louis, there is a simple Latin cross suspended above the altar with a slender, serpentine-looking corpus attached to it. A processional cross was designed as a smaller replica of this eye-catching artistic centerpiece. With ornate stained glass windows in the background depicting the chapel's namesake preachers and symbols of the Means of Grace, this stylized crucifix certainly stands out. John 3:14 may in fact be Scripture's only explicit connection of Christ's crucifixion to Moses' serpent, but it serves as the inspiration for those who gather in this particular sacred space to keep our eyes fixed on Jesus, firm in the faith that trusts in the gift of eternal life paid for by His shed blood.

Shortly after his brother Aaron died, Moses was subjected to yet another round of Israelite grumbling—you know, no food, no water, why did you take us out of Egypt?—that sort of thing again. Their only way into the Promised Land was to go through Edom, and they were blocked by an uncooperative king who was unafraid to use his own army to stop them. Before they could keep going north, Israel had to go south to get around the descendants of Esau. This time, the Lord responded to their complaints when He sent the fiery serpents—perhaps they looked red like fire or their bites felt fiery hot with venom. Many people died, many more were at death's door with the fatal poison.

God told Moses to craft a bronze serpent and set it up high on a pole, so that those who still believed in the power of the divine Word would look up to the crucified snake and be healed. It wasn't the brazen form itself that had any ability to heal; it was God's promise to save that came through instead, together with the contrite admission of sin and priestly prayer of Moses on the people's behalf. Even so, the bronze serpent lingered in Israel's possession for centuries, through the time of the Judges, King David, all the way down the line to good King Hezekiah, who destroyed the relic that had eventually become the object of pagan worship among an Israelite people who had been too apt to stray.

Looking up to Christ is not merely trying to follow the example He led in keeping all the commandments perfectly. It means to regard our Savior just as Moses wanted Israel to regard the Lord's promise concerning the bronze serpent: (Numbers 21:8)"Everyone who is bitten, when he sees it, shall live." So too, the Christian who often finds himself bitten near to death with the attacks of Satan, the world, and his own sinful nature, that penitent believer can now proclaim with joy, "My faith looks up to Thee, Thou Lamb of Calvary, Savior divine" (*LSB* 702:1).

5 Wilderness Battles and Talking Donkeys (Numbers 21–25; 31)

Finally, the people of Israel began advancing north, preparing to put an end to their forty years of wandering and set foot in the Promised Land. As they emerged from the rugged desert, they encountered more populated areas—cities and kings instead of occasional nomads, such as Moses' father-in-law Jethro. Their route took them along the King's Highway, a route that followed the massive rift in that region's geography, passing along the east edge of the Dead Sea. Having once been in mountainous terrain on the Sinai Peninsula, now they were in valleys well below sea level. This highway was the easiest, most direct route from the tip of the Red Sea's Gulf of Aqaba (at the modern-day city of Eilat) due north all the way to Damascus, which is past the Jordan River and the Sea of Galilee (called the Sea of Chinnereth in Old Testament times). A freeway, most of it four lanes, exists along a significant part of this route today, a major artery for the country of Jordan.

Two kings would not let Israel pass through this area without a fight. They saw the two million people and were either intimidated enough to strike first before they got any closer, or they thought they could pounce upon the weaknesses of so large a traveling party. Just over the border from Moab on their way north, the Israelites engaged the first king, Sihon, who ruled over the Amorites living in the territory that they had just entered. Upon their decisive victory at Jahaz, Israel dispossessed the Amorites of all their western land and, through His people, the Lord brought down upon that heathen nation the judgment He had vowed to Abraham that He would render, once their iniquity reached the limit of God's forbearance (Genesis 15:16).

Pushing farther north, the elevation begins to rise again, and Israel entered the more fertile heights of Gilead and Bashan. Here is where the second king, the giant Og, opposed them and was also defeated, his people being devoted to complete destruction. Success such as this started gaining the notice of other nations and kings, so Balak, king of Moab, responded with a different tactic to try to defeat Israel. He hired a holy man, Balaam, to curse this invading horde instead. The Lord twice deterred Balaam from accepting the offer, the second time even using his donkey to speak some sense into him! Wisely, Balaam ended up choosing not to fall for the riches and honor that the Moabite king offered him, but instead resolved, (Numbers 22:38) "The word that God puts in my mouth, that must I speak." And whereas Balak insisted that Balaam curse the Lord's chosen people, the Lord gave Balaam blessings to pronounce instead.

Conclusion

The Book of Numbers is a transitional book, as indicated by the two different reasons for the censuses that occur at its beginning and near its end. The children of Israel move from their wandering home of forty years in the wilderness to get themselves finally in position to cross over the Jordan River into the Promised Land. But before they can get there, they have lessons of faithfulness to learn, battles to fight for the Lord, and blessings to receive from a man who was paid to curse. This is the beginning of the end for Moses and his leadership of this massive traveling nation, but a new leader is arising in Joshua, in whom we see a pattern for the greater Joshua, our Savior, Jesus Christ.

Concluding Activities

Speak a closing prayer, make any necessary announcements, and distribute study leaflet 9.

Planning to Settle

Leviticus 26–27; Numbers 13; 32–36; Deuteronomy 1–4; 9–11; 19–34

Preparing for the Session

Central Focus

Turning our attention to the Book of Deuteronomy, we recount the forty years of wandering in the desert as they come to an end. Here the Law is restated, past events are rehashed, and the groundwork is laid for the future of God's people. By the time Moses says his good-bye and Joshua summons his courage to take over, we will have a good idea ourselves of our Lord's Torah instruction and how we may apply it faithfully in our walk with Christ as we journey to the future, heavenly promised land.

Objectives

That participants, led by the Holy Spirit working through God's Word, will

1. recall the Israelite tribes who did not settle in the Promised Land itself, and why;
2. find the promised land in all its details fulfilled in Jesus Christ; and
3. shine brightly as a blessing and witness of the true faith to our neighbor.

Note for the small-group leaders: Lesson notes and other materials you will need begin on page 85.

For the Lecture Leader Session Plan

Worship

Begin the session with the hymn printed in the study leaflet. Accompaniments are available in denominational hymnals, such as *Lutheran Service Book* or *Lutheran Worship* (refer to hymnal index). (Note: Concordia Publishing House has available *The Concordia Organist.* All the initial worship hymns in the LifeLight courses are included in this resource. It's especially helpful for mission congregations and small parishes. See the list of study resources on page 7.) Follow with this prayer:

Prayer

O God and Father of our Lord Jesus Christ, in Your love and mercy, You delivered Your people from forty years in the desert and finally brought them under Your servant Joshua to the land of their promised inheritance. Help and guide us constantly in our spiritual journey, for we know not where we go; however, by grace, we are confident that You are there with us, with Your everlasting arms underneath us. Lead us from our sin to the cross; to the empty tomb; to the pulpit, font, and altar; and finally, to our grave. At every turn, help us witness to Your love and instruction, as well as testify to Your forgiveness and everlasting peace; through the same Jesus Christ, Your Son, our Lord. Amen.

Lecture Presentation

1 Reuben and Gad (Numbers 13; 32; Deuteronomy 3)

With Israel's initial battle successes over the kings Sihon and Og, God's people entered a new phase in their history as a nation. From wandering in the wilderness, their thoughts finally turned toward settling the lands that flowed with milk and honey. Because the Lord's hand was behind it all, the conquests of lands east of the Jordan River seemed easy. The enemies were wiped out, the cities and lands and possessions were handed to the weary wanderers on a silver platter.

That's what might have caught the eye of the people belonging to the tribes of Reuben and Gad. They had numerous flocks and herds, and for forty years, transportation was a significant issue for them. As the verdant, rolling hills of Gilead and Bashan lay before them without anyone to claim them, these two tribes sought their opportunity to settle prior to crossing the Jordan into the Promised Land of Canaan. Their representatives came to Moses and the chieftains under him to secure for themselves the first pick from the land that Israel had just conquered.

But before Moses would agree to hand over this land to Reuben and Gad, he needed to clarify something. It was the request (Numbers 32:5) "Do not take us across the Jordan" that must have raised his eyebrow. Moses had seen this before, and he was a good judge of the lethargic tendencies of the sinful human nature. Back when he sent those twelve spies into the land of Canaan, they toured the land for forty days and brought back not only heavy clusters of luscious grapes, but also a bunch of frightful stories of giants and their fortified strongholds. Only Caleb and Joshua recalled that the Lord's mighty arm would destroy these enemies and deliver these lands to Israel. And since the whole people listened to the bad news rather than the good news of God's promise, they were consigned to forty years of wandering, based on the forty days of spying.

With that whole episode still in the back of his mind, Moses required a vow from the representatives of the tribes of Reuben and Gad to have their fighting men cross the Jordan and help their relatives in the ten other tribes gain their own lands in Canaan. Then they would be allowed to return and settle in their eastern inheritance. The first shall be last. They promised Moses not to let down the rest of the people Israel; they would fight to secure the lands that lay to the west. Moses was pleased, and added only one thing to what they vowed: their obligation was not merely to their relatives in the other tribes, but especially to the Lord, their God. They should never forget that the battles are His, because the inheritance of land would come solely from the hand of the Almighty. The officially announced agreement included a short period of time for these fighting men to set up permanent dwellings for their noncombatants and pens for their animals, and then they would cross over the Jordan to fulfill their vow.

Also, a third group was added to the tribes of Reuben and Gad so that they, too, would share with them the lands that were formerly under the control of Amorite kings. This was a portion of the tribe of Manasseh, son of Joseph. This "half-tribe" was comprised of those clans of warriors who were instrumental in defeating the Amorites and capturing certain areas of Gilead. In recognition for their efforts, they will participate in the "settlement" reached with Reuben and Gad. The other half of the tribe of Manasseh would receive land in Canaan, under the leadership of Joshua.

This chapter in Israel's history would have wrapped up neatly several years later, were it not for one more misunderstanding that would threaten the delicate balance of intertribal peace. In Joshua 22, the fighting men from Reuben, Gad, and the half-tribe of Manasseh fulfilled their promise. They fought the battles with Joshua and the rest of their relatives, so that all twelve tribes finally had their land. On their way back east across the Jordan, these two and a half tribes paved the way for their future generations to worship the one true God who had given them such rich blessings. They constructed an altar, impressive in size and modeled after the altar that had been erected at the Lord's permanent site for His tabernacle in Canaan. The nine other tribes, plus the Manassites who settled west of the Jordan, assumed that these easterners were going to use this altar in a plan to break off from them and reject the Lord's prescribed sacrifices. Thankfully, they were allowed to explain themselves, and they clearly asserted that they had no such intentions. The people of Reuben, Gad, and East-Manasseh built this witness altar merely to remind future generations that even though the Jordan River divided them, the gifts of the Lord's Divine Service at His one true altar of sacrifice are meant for all believers, no matter where they lived.

2 Where We've Been (Numbers 33; skim Deuteronomy 1–4; 9–11)

Moses wrote down more than just the Ten Commandments, of course. He also kept a detailed travel log that covered Israel's entire journey through the wilderness. He did not write this to merely pass the time. No, Moses received orders from the Lord Himself to write down where His people had been, and record each place where they had set up their camp for the time being. Recall that all of their movement across the desert was determined by the pillar of cloud and fire, and whether the Lord lifted the cloud and moved on or He let His presence remain in the same place over the tent of meeting. With every new campsite, God was at work among His people, and His gracious promise was continually brought to their attention. The whole nation picked up and moved somewhat regularly during their forty years of wandering. For that reason alone, Numbers 33 turns out to be a hefty collection of location names that are usually quite difficult to pronounce!

This tiny forty-year slice of Israel's national history became just as essential to their success as were God's stone tablets of the Law. For one thing, with every new generation since the exodus, the mighty act of salvation in Egypt receded farther and farther into the back of the people's collective mind. Even as the Passover festival endeavored to ensure that this all-important past event stayed fresh, the tendency would always be there to forget all that God had done to save His people.

Another benefit that comes from this recorded collection of campsites was an invigorated worship life. Confident of the presence of the Lord as He accompanied the congregation throughout their marching, the people chanted praises for His wonderful works. This liturgy began with the words that Moses sang when they broke camp and left a place behind: (Numbers 10:35) "Arise, O Lord, and let Your enemies be scattered, and let those who hate You flee before You." At the end of a particular stage of the journey, when the cloudy pillar ceased to go on farther, Moses then chanted, (v. 36) "Return, O Lord, to the ten thousand thousands of Israel." Some similar musical pieces about this wilderness period are still found in several Psalms that recap Israel's journey, such as 78, 81, 83, 95, 105, 106, 135, and 136.

Finally, Moses recalled the story of the Israelites' wilderness wanderings by means of an extended sermon. This work of historical commentary has been recorded in Deuteronomy, which was pointed out in the first week of our study as the "second-giving" of the Law. This, of course, does not mean more rules to follow and hoops to jump through. The *Torah*, or Law of God, is His full instruction—Law *and* Gospel, if you will—that inspires faith in the new generations that will henceforth occupy the inheritance that was promised to their fathers, going all the way back to Abraham. Moses retold God's story with regard to His people, adding explanations and Holy Spirit-inspired comments that were expressly intended for the faithful edification of his congregation. A similar historical "rewrite" was affected by the author of 1 and 2 Chronicles, because the history he covered had already been written down in previous books—he was similarly inspired to use that raw material to teach future generations what the Lord had been doing among them all along the way. Sometimes, He worked through His people; other times, it was in spite of them.

3 Setting Boundaries and Tithes (Numbers 34–36; Deuteronomy 19–20; 26)

Once the new generation of Israel's twelve tribes was counted in the census of Numbers 26, the land of Canaan could be divided up into their respective portions. With a cartographer's detail, the Lord spelled out clearly for Moses all the borders and land parcels that they would inherit, and this before anyone else had even set eyes on a single bit of its dirt! The Bible critic cries foul at this point and simply assumes that this portion of Scripture could not have been recorded with this much specificity until long after Israel had settled in Canaan. But who was it that granted Moses the ability, before his death, to see in a moment of time the entire land that was promised to Abraham? None other than the Lord God Almighty! He was the one who drew up the map, so to speak, that would direct Joshua and the other leaders who had drawn lots for their respective tribes' land holdings. Property markers that would be set down according to the established directions were protected from removal almost as if they were holy shrines, because if one dishonestly increased their allotted land, that would be an offense against the true owner of the land—God the Lord.

Since the Levites were not going to receive a chunk of Promised Land like the others, they would be assigned certain cities from the lands of each of their fellow tribes. Again, the census figures would be used to determine the proportionate number of cities that each tribe would hand over. They would inhabit forty-two cities as their own, plus a little more than a quarter mile of pastureland encircling each city gate. To the Levites would also belong six special cities evenly spaced from one another, three to the east of the Jordan River and three to the west. These would be known as cities of refuge—safe zones, you could say—for anyone who accidentally shed blood. The Lord's strict protection of the sanctity of life, given in the rule recorded in Genesis 9:6, is not going to be set aside, even when that death is not intentional. Instead, the manslayer who is truly innocent of any premeditation, and thus not a transgressor of the Fifth Commandment, can remain alive and out of the reach of any avenger while inside the walls of the city of refuge. The only event that would release him to return to his own land is the death of the high priest. Not even the jubilee year can atone for the shedding of blood. Of course, if the murder is intentional and it can be demonstrated that it was carried out in anger or with a weapon that could cause death, then not even a city of refuge will protect the assailant—his life is required at the hand of an avenger.

How can something like this be proven? You need witnesses, as in more than one. Here in Deuteronomy, we have the rule that Christ Himself quotes in Matthew 18: "Every charge may be established by the evidence of two or three witnesses." Paul takes the hint and promotes this procedure in early Christian congregations as a lawful and wise course of action (2 Corinthians 13:1; 1 Timothy 5:19). The malicious lone false witness deserves to be purged from God's holy people.

One of the last commands that Moses passed down from the Lord concerned that which will be given to Him first. A tithe is tied to the Promised Land because it will be paid from the harvest that this very ground will yield each year. It was commanded to provide for the Levite's role in preparing God's people for the coming of Christ, and to set a good example for all times that believers are to care for the less fortunate. Even though we lack a specific tithing commandment in our New Testament time, we have something even better in the freedom of the Gospel: (2 Corinthians 9:7) "Each one must give as he has decided in his heart, not reluctantly or under compulsion, for God loves a cheerful giver."

4 Blessings and Curses (Leviticus 26–27; Deuteronomy 21; 27–29)

Archaeologists have found several examples of agreements and covenants from the ancient Near East, and they include conditions and obligations placed upon each party as well as an advance invocation of a curse if the covenant is broken. A similarity or two can certainly be noted when you compare them with God's covenant that He has made with His chosen people Israel; however, one should not get too carried away. This is no ordinary compact between a lord and a vassal, and it's certainly not an equilateral agreement struck by two neighboring parties. Instead, we have the one-way promise granted by the Creator of heaven and earth to lonely Abraham, and the unlikely prospects of children, land, and communion with the divine. There can hardly be any conditions on Israel's part that can hold a candle to God's side of the bargain!

Rather than characterizing God's covenant on one hand as some stale gentlemen's agreement, nor on the other hand as a list of demands that would earn His favor, it would be more accurate to speak in terms of His grace and desire to dwell among His people. Obedience to the Lord's commands is a demonstration of faith, indicating a receptivity to His blessing that is always there. Just as the Small Catechism teaches with respect to the petition "Give us this day our daily bread," we learn from Scripture that God has already given everything needed in this body and life to everyone, even to all evil people, but we still pray that He would lead us to realize this ourselves and receive His blessings with a thankful heart.

On the flip side, the curses for disobedience are best understood as the Lord's warning about what the specific actions are that will stand as roadblocks on the avenue of His grace toward Israel. Dr. Kleinig explains that when God's people wandered away from His covenant, whether in the moral, civic, or ceremonial spheres, "They did not terminate it by their disobedience, for no human being could ever undo what God had done. Instead, they frustrated its operation, so that God could not accomplish what He intended through it. By their disobedience they forfeited the blessings of God's covenant; they experienced the threatened consequences of their faithlessness to God" (*Leviticus*, p. 574). This is the Lord's alien work; that is, although the Lord does not shove people away in anger—preferring instead to bestow abundant blessings on them—in His love, He makes His people fully aware of anything that might creep in to destroy their faith.

His chastisement follows certain steps or grades of admonition, beginning with panic, disease, and harassment at the hands of enemies. If faithlessness stubbornly continues in spite of all the increasing intensities of punishments, the final blow threatened from the hand of the Lord will be exile (and yes, this fate was predicted *and written down* centuries before it really happened). However, even with such a drastic measure, God's grace will still win out. In the event of an exile, the people will be removed from the land only long enough for its required period of Sabbath rest. Then, at just the right time, the Lord will "remember" His covenant, just as He had "remembered" His people in Egypt, lift their curse, and bring them back to the land of His promise.

There was only one covenant curse that was not reversed, which was God's design from the very beginning. That was the ultimate curse of wrath against all sin that was unleashed upon Jesus Christ, our Savior. He bore that curse for us, suffered the bloody pain and the shame, and along with all of that, God the Son in human flesh fell under the heavenly Father's curse upon Him by being hanged on the tree of the cross (Deuteronomy 21:23). But with His glorious resurrection from the dead on the third day, Christ has set up a new covenant of one-way blessing—the Means of Grace whereby His Church will receive unbounded forgiveness and certain hope of eternal life. Instead of a narrow plot of land, our inheritance is even greater in the new creation. Along with Moses, Abraham, David, and all the heavenly host, we will see the Lord face-to-face, even though He is already among us in His Word, in Baptism, and in Holy Communion.

5 Moses' Final Days (Deuteronomy 30–34)

The great Lawgiver, Moses, has reached the Promised Land's border, and he leaves the children of Israel with a series of Gospel promises and blessings. All of his writing has been for the benefit of them and many generations after them. Once the blessings and curses have been spelled out—those two ways of life and death that lie before us all—the fearless prophet without equal entreats his flock to choose life, to follow the ways of the Lord, hold fast to Him, and dwell in the land of His unending blessing.

As he hands over the reins of leadership to Joshua, Moses reminds the people that even though he will not be there physically with them in the Promised Land, his words will continue on as a witness. Every seven years at the Feast of Booths, that liturgical reminder of their life spent in tents, the priests are required to read the Book of the Law. He taught them a song, "Give ear, O heavens" (Deuteronomy 32:1–43), to extol the power and love of the Lord as well as to warn them of His jealous anger. By the Word of the Lord alone will God's people live in the land of their inheritance and enjoy His blessing.

With a final word addressed to each of Israel's tribes, Moses takes his leave to ascend a mountain for the last time. This time, he mounts the summit of Pisgah in order to be granted his promised view of Canaan. (*LSB* 798:6) "The goodly land I see, With peace and plenty blest: A land of sacred liberty And endless rest. There milk and honey flow, And oil and wine abound, And trees of life forever grow With mercy crowned." What Moses could only see from afar, the people conquered by the mighty hand of the Lord. But none of them have the vantage point that the baptized Christian has, because our Savior has ushered us into the final promised land of eternal salvation. We have been granted a promised inheritance in the new heavens and new earth that will never pass away.

After his death, Moses had an opportunity to visit the land that during his life he was forbidden to tread. At the transfiguration of Jesus (Luke 9:28–36), Moses and Elijah appeared to speak with Jesus about His departure, that is, His exodus, "which He was about to accomplish at Jerusalem" (v. 31). So, on another mountain height, this time inside the Promised Land's borders, the leader of the first exodus, by which the Lord brought release to Israelite captives, joined with the prophet who had been taken in a whirlwind up to heaven to discuss the great, once-for-all exodus to liberate the entire world from the slavery to sin.

Conclusion

The time of wandering in the wilderness came to an end, but the history of Israel was about to enter into a new chapter. Disobedience to the Lord's commandments and rejection of His love seem tragically imminent, yet not even that diminishes the abundance of love and blessing that await His people. Though they fall away, He will never forget His promises; His forgiving mercy never fails. And we pray for that day when we, too, will see for ourselves that which we possess now by faith in Christ. Come, Lord Jesus!

Concluding Activities

Speak a closing prayer, make any necessary announcements, and announce the next *LifeLight* topic.

Small-Group Leaders Material

How Did We Get Here?

Exodus; Numbers 7–9; 11; 13–14; Deuteronomy 5–8

Preparing for the Session

Central Focus

This session serves as an introduction to the wilderness wanderings of the Israelites, touching briefly on the exodus from Egypt and setting the stage for the forty years that follow it. Given this context, a clearer light can then shine upon the last three Books of Moses.

Objectives

That participants, led by the Holy Spirit working through God's Word, will

1. review the exodus and the actions of the Israelites immediately following;
2. take note of the significance of these early events to the current study; and
3. be able to relate these events to further study of Leviticus, Numbers, and Deuteronomy.

For the Small-Group Leader

Small-Group Discussion Helps

Day 1 • Exodus 12; Numbers 9:1–14

1. The Israelites' first sign of faith in the Lord's act of deliverance was the slaughter of the unblemished lamb. Aside from being a clear type and prediction of Christ, the lamb was the centerpiece of the Passover event. It must be roasted; its blood must mark the doors of the faithful; and it is to be fully consumed or burned by morning. Other signs of faith would be for the people to eat the Passover ready to travel, the bitter herbs, and the unleavened bread.

2. Genesis 1 describes a day as "there was evening and there was morning." So a new day was reckoned in the Bible to begin at sundown or "twilight." The Passover ritual begins on the very day that the Lord leads His people out of slavery. The Lord's Supper, which is the fulfillment of Passover, occurs also at sundown on what we know as Holy (Maundy) Thursday, which makes it the very same day as when our Savior, Jesus, died on the cross to rescue the world from slavery to sin.

3. Unleavened bread was quicker to make, and it allowed for the Israelites to get up and travel out of Egypt at a moment's notice. As the verses point out, they were left without any time to let bread dough rise—they had to eat the Passover meal "in haste." Theologically, yeast was given the significance of impurity, of a threat to the community as a unified whole, of the spread of evil among the holy, starting with a little bit, and then working throughout the whole lump of dough. Paul definitely has this meaning in mind as he speaks about proper church discipline in the congregation at Corinth.

4. Answers may vary. Center the discussion on key events that the Israelites would have recalled as they relived the exodus in the elements of the Passover festival. You could perhaps ask the group, "Would the events that they would most likely recall necessarily be the most spectacular moments, or would something more mundane be just as likely to stick in their memories? Why?"

5. God's judgment on the gods of Egypt through the plagues, especially the final plague, is to expose them as false gods, worthless to help those who call on them for help. The angel of death will visit every unbelieving household with the death of the firstborn. Rather than being gods, these idols are actually demons, as pointed out in Deuteronomy and 1 Corinthians. For us today, the Lord's judgment on false gods includes a plea for us to remain faithful to Him and to rely on His providence for all that we need. This refers us back to the requirements of the First Commandment: You shall have no other gods.

Day 2 • Exodus 23:20–33; Numbers 13–14

6. The Lord promised Abraham (Abram) both a multitude of descendants and the possession of the Promised Land itself: the land of Canaan. Remember that Moses, by divine inspiration, has already written or is writing down the Book of Genesis by the time the Israelites' journey takes place.

7. The commands of Exodus 23 are written with the assumption that God's people will most certainly take possession of Canaan. The First Commandment, "You shall have no other gods," is seen throughout, especially in the prohibition of worship toward the defeated gods of the Promised Land's current inhabitants. The fruits of faith, including the observance of civil and ceremonial laws in this chapter and throughout the Pentateuch, will demonstrate the people's adherence to this foundational commandment.

8. When the Israelites finally arrive in Canaan, they will work systematically to drive out the inhabitants as they increase in number and move throughout the land of God's promise. It won't happen all at once, "lest the land become desolate and the wild beasts multiply against you" (Exodus 23:29). Wild beasts denote a creation in disarray, a sign of wilderness chaos instigated by the devil to try to shake an otherwise solid faith (see Mark 1:13).

9. Upon the return of the twelve spies who were sent into Canaan, the people were afraid of the mighty Canaanites and their superior strength and defense. This was a clear statement of their lack of faith and trust in God. They were not ready to enter the Promised Land. The two spies who insisted that the Lord would fulfill His Word, namely Caleb and Joshua, would be the only ones of that generation to enter the land that they saw. The other so-called able-bodied men numbered in the census would end their lives wandering in the wilderness. Ironically, their "little ones"—the very ones whom they feared would be vulnerable to attack and defeat at the hands of these frightening giants—would end up as the victorious conquerors.

10. The creedal statement in Numbers 14:18—as well as in Psalm 103:8, Joel 2:13, and even Jonah 4:2—is centered on the Lord's forgiveness. This is at the heart of the Christian confession, justification by grace through faith. Assist the students in expressing their statements, and help them affirm a firm, certain hope in forgiveness and salvation through Christ alone.

Day 3 • Skim Exodus 16–17; read Numbers 11

11. The manna was given to the children of Israel during the second month following the exodus from Egypt because of their grumbling against Moses and Aaron, which is really grumbling against the Lord Himself. Of course, the manna was a daily reminder that God provides for all our physical needs (review what the Small Catechism says about the Fourth Petition of the Lord's Prayer). The spiritual teaching involved cultivating their faith in Him, as Deuteronomy 8:3 records and Jesus repeats, "Man does not live by bread alone, but man lives by every word that comes from the mouth of the LORD."

12. The manna came to an end when the Israelites were able to eat of the produce of the Promised Land. It was meant to carry them through their forty-year journey only. God still would always provide all they needed to support their body and life; He was simply going to switch to a different means of doing it. As an everlasting testimony, the jar of manna that was kept before the Presence of the Lord would perpetuate this heavenly bread's spiritual lesson.

13. Moses at first was commanded by the Lord at Meribah to strike the rock in order to produce water for the people of Israel to drink. God again provided for earthly needs, but He did so in order to awaken faith in their hearts. As St. Paul notes in 1 Corinthians 10, Christ the spiritual Rock followed them, so that they could drink from (that is, believe in) Him. Their constant struggle of faith is useful instruction for us Christians today as we seek to cultivate a healthy life of repentance.

14. In Numbers 11, the grumbling of the Israelites is reflected in Moses' conversation with the Lord. To be sure, he had the privilege to speak face-to-face with God, but now he is clearly taking issue and asking some hard questions. He is not defiant; rather, in faith, Moses speaks, drastic though it may sound (especially in v. 15), confident that the Lord will answer him in mercy.

15. It is all too common these days among Christians to reason in some way that "God wants me to be happy, so if I am not being blessed in the way I want, then I have to do something about it." Prosperity of God's people in the Old Testament does not necessarily translate into a guarantee of material blessings for us today. It remains true that all things come from His hand, and like Job, we need to learn the hard lesson that we take the bad along with the good (Job 2:10). If we deceive ourselves into thinking that there is something we do in order to open our Lord's hand of blessing upon us, or that a difficult trial is a punishment sent from the Lord against us, then we are lured into the temptation of works righteousness. Faith becomes strong when it endures suffering and looks not to earthly blessings but to the heavenly city of which we are citizens by God's grace to us in Christ.

Day 4 • Skim Exodus 13; 26; 40; Numbers 7–9

16. God signals His presence in these passages through the pillar of cloud and pillar of fire. He establishes a covenant with Abraham, rescues the children of Israel from Pharaoh and his army, and surrounds first Mount Sinai and later the tabernacle, each time employing the same cloud. This assures the Israelites that the Lord Himself will lead them, and He will let them know when it is time to move on, but most especially that the people can trust in His ability to keep His promises, even though they nevertheless often doubt and complain.

17. The "glory of the Lord" and the cloud theophanies in Scripture occur at important times when God's gracious presence is especially emphasized. This appearance is truly other-worldly, especially in the detail with which it is described in Ezekiel 1, so naturally it would inspire fear in those who beheld such a sight. In addition to this, the Lord's absolute glory is an utter threat to sinful flesh—Moses needed to be covered in the rock cleft so that he would see only God's back; Isaiah mourned over his lack of clean lips. But the Lord also atones for this utter lack of holiness so that His glory does not destroy man, but rather saves him.

18. Each of the twelve tribes (excluding Levi, but making Joseph into two: Ephraim and Manasseh) offers the same dedicatory gift at the tabernacle, proceeding in the same order as their camps are designated in Numbers 2. The tribe of Judah takes the lead, and as the genealogy in Matthew reveals, Judah is the tribe from which the Christ will be born in the fullness of time. This priority also could refer to Genesis 49:10 and Judah's "scepter," the kingly line that would include David, who is also an ancestor of Jesus according to the flesh.

19. The Kohathites are given the singular privilege of carrying the holy vessels and furnishings, such as the ark, altar, and lampstand, which are found in and near the tabernacle. They may not touch them, however, nor prepare them for travel, or else they will die; their relatives the priests are the ones expressly given that role, since it is their assigned work to use them when the tabernacle is set up in the camp.

20. Answers may vary. Most people would probably note a difference in their reaction if they were suddenly to see a visible revelation of God's glory. Such an unmistakable assurance of His presence may seem to be advantageous in promoting greater devotion to the Lord, since His "hiddenness" often leads many people to take His gifts for granted. But along with our Lord's using lowly means to communicate His gracious presence, He also grants us faith by the power of the Holy Spirit, so that it remains true for us: "Blessed are those who have not seen and yet have believed" (John 20:29).

Day 5 • Exodus 20; Deuteronomy 5–8

21. The Ten Commandments begin with the Lord stating who He is and what He has done for His people. His demands that are laid out in the Law are based on His salvation and are meant to describe the fruits of faith in Him, rather than as a set of conditions for Israel to fulfill. He is the Creator, who was separated from us by sin; yet He overcame the enemy that enslaved us and carried us through to His promised inheritance of heaven. Through Christ, the loving relationship that was begun with the Israelites long ago is also established with us by faith today.

22. Moses recalls how the people first received this Law from God on Mount Sinai, and he noted how God's voice, the fire, the cloud, and the thick darkness inspired great fear in the multitude. In verse 29, Moses quotes the Lord, "Oh that they had such a heart as this always, to fear Me and to keep all My commandments . . . !" A holy and righteous fear of God is centered not only on the fear of punishment but also on the reverence and grateful awe inspired by His almighty power to save. When Israel disregarded the Lord and lacked this kind of fear, then they rebelled and turned to idols, grumbling, and all other kinds of wickedness.

23. Parents are charged specifically to teach the commands and repeat the history of the Lord's salvation to their children. This duty is to be foremost in their minds at all times of the day, inscribed with prominence everywhere, even on their own bodies, so that God's Word is with them constantly at home and at work. For us today, this priority is best understood as a real need to teach the faith to our own and following generations. We do this as we attend worship services, read Scripture, pray, study the catechism, confess our sins and receive absolution, and take part in regular conversations about matters that require the application of God's Word.

24. God's command that the false gods should be "devoted to destruction" is the flip side of setting aside something to be holy. In other words, because of the Lord's promise to His own people, because the pagan nations' sins have finally reached full measure (see Genesis 15:16), and in order to prevent their idolatry from infiltrating the holy people, His wrath will be unleashed against these enemies through complete annihilation and destruction. Similar to the destruction by means of a flood in Noah's day, everything and everyone opposed to God is to be wiped out. This "devotion" is an act of worship and obedience; the military conquest is understood to be an offering. When the land was secured for God's holy people, His destruction command was removed. It had done its appointed work to prepare for the coming kingdom of the Messiah, who comes "not by might, nor by power, but by My Spirit, says the LORD of hosts" (Zechariah 4:6).

25. Riches and wealth are not forbidden in Deuteronomy, nor does the mere presence of them guarantee that one will be led astray. The great resources of the Promised Land will certainly bring wealth to God's people once they arrive there, but the real point of this portion of Moses' sermon is for the Israelites' faith to remain strong, in times of prosperity as well as in need. The temptation with riches will always be to put trust in them and to say in one's heart: "My power and the might of my hand have gotten me this wealth" (Deuteronomy 8:17). This self-idolatry that can attach itself to worldly things is the impetus for this exhortation and for Christ's statement about the rich man in the Gospels. The remedy is supplied by Moses in Deuteronomy 8:18: "You shall remember the LORD your God, for it is He who gives you power to get wealth." He not only gives wealth but also the true riches of eternal life in Christ.

Making Offerings

Leviticus 1–5; Numbers 28–29

Preparing for the Session

Central Focus

Leviticus begins with an in-depth look at the worship life of God's people in the Old Testament. The various offerings that are prescribed at the beginning of the book provide a constant reminder of our total dependence on our merciful, heavenly Father.

Objectives

That participants, led by the Holy Spirit working through God's Word, will

1. identify and differentiate five particular offerings described in Leviticus;
2. find how these offerings fit in to the Lord's ceremonial worship plan of the Old Testament; and
3. relate these offerings to their fulfillment in Christ and the New Testament.

For the Small-Group Leader

Small-Group Discussion Helps

Day 1 • Leviticus 1; Numbers 28:1–10

1. The burnt offering begins with a male from the herd, that is, a bull, without blemish. The next choice could be a perfect firstborn male from the flock, either a sheep or a goat. Finally, a burnt offering of birds, either turtledoves or pigeons, without explicit reference to the sex of the bird, is allowed under the commandment of the Lord. The progression seems to go from larger to smaller, in size and in value, and perhaps the most advisable offering of the three categories is that of the bull, given that it is first on the list.

2. In the description of offering a bull for a burnt offering, the person making the offering places his hand on the head of the animal prior to sacrificing it. This ritual is not spoken of in exactly the same way as the scapegoat is in Leviticus 16:21, where the sins of the people are explicitly listed with the laying on of hands. The ceremony remains for the offering-giver, however, as a form of identification with the animal, so that the burnt offering makes specific atonement for him.

3. The priest (or son of Aaron) assists in the sacrifice but does not act until the blood of the animal is ready to be poured out. The person offering the sacrifice is called upon to kill the bull, sheep, or goat. The priest then collects the blood and throws it upon the bronze altar. He washes the legs and entrails so that all parts of the carcass are ensured worthy to be placed on top of the altar. Placing the sliced animal into the fire on the altar is also the responsibility of the priest. In the case of a bird being offered as a burnt offering, the priest is given the command to wring its neck and remove the unclean parts.

4. The tent was how God revealed His gracious presence among His people. He was not distant, reserved to a mountain, but instead was right in the middle of the Israelite tribes and their camps. In John 1, Jesus is described as the Word of God who became flesh and "dwelt among us" (v. 14). This phrase means that Jesus lived and walked here on earth among His own creatures in the better tent of His perfect, human body, instead of the shadow tent that was prescribed in the Old Testament. He is the tabernacle, or temple, the true interaction of God with men.

5. The burnt offering, as with several other offerings by fire that are described in Leviticus, becomes a "pleasing aroma" or "food offering" accepted by the Lord. This is known as an anthropomorphism, an instance where a human activity or attribute is applied to God. The point of this worship term is to say that the faith by which the believer offers the offering to the Lord is what makes it pleasing to Him. The burning flesh and sacrificed meat are nothing if they are not accompanied by faith in the real sacrifice of the real Lamb of God who takes away the sin of the world, namely Jesus.

Day 2 • Leviticus 2; Numbers 28:11–15

6. The second chapter of Leviticus turns from animal sacrifices in the burnt offerings to the offering of grain before the priest over and above the regular tithe. Sin and atonement are not incorporated in this ceremony, as they are in chapter 1. The burnt offering was entirely

obliterated, since it was exclusively meant for the Lord. Now, with the grain offering (as with other similar offerings), a portion will be burned, and the rest will be reserved for the priests. There is a similarity in that the grain offering needs to be the best, just as the burnt offering has to be selected from among the unblemished males of the species.

7. The grain offering includes a portion that is set aside for the priests, or "Aaron's sons," to eat while standing in the court area around the tent of meeting. This firstfruits quality flour or roasted grain is unleavened, mixed together with olive oil, topped with frankincense, and seasoned with salt to identify its holy character. A portion is designated as a "memorial" that is burned as a "pleasing aroma" to the Lord.

8. The offering of firstfruits comes in connection with the celebration of Passover and the week-long Feast of Unleavened Bread. It was offered up in part out of thankfulness for the salvation that the Lord accomplished for the Israelites in bringing them up out of Egypt. The fiftieth day after the Feast of Firstfruits was also observed as the Feast of Weeks, or Pentecost. We observe the giving or tithing of our firstfruits as Christians because, by faith, we regard all that we have, including especially the salvation that is ours in Christ, as a gift from the Lord's generous hand, entrusted to us for our use as His stewards.

9. Cain made an offering of grain, or according to the Scripture, "of the fruit of the ground." His offering is contrasted with Abel's offering of the firstborn of the flock, but the difference isn't really in what was sacrificed but in the *faith* through which the sacrifice was offered to the Lord. Hebrews 11 helps clear this up and commends the faith of Abel among that of many others who trusted in God's promises along with their various actions that expressed that faith. That is what He regards when we do anything in our worship practice or daily vocation.

10. In Psalm 50, the criticism is leveled against using sacrifices as a cover-up for false faith. The sacrifices are not the issue; it is the evil that is being promoted through the conduct of those who "forget God." No amount of ceremonial sacrifices can make up for a hardened, unrepentant, immoral life. Our Creator does not need the sacrifices anyway; He is not waiting with bated breath for our worship to complete Him in some way. A feigned sacrifice is dangerous because then it becomes a false hope, or even an idol. Faith is what is required, and it comes as a gift freely from the Lord's hand.

Day 3 • Leviticus 3

11. The order of animal species is the same for bringing a burnt offering, but for the peace offering, a male or female is allowed. The unblemished animal is killed by the one bringing the offering, who lays his hand on its head, and its blood is thrown against the four sides of the altar of burnt offering. In this chapter, the fat and inner organs of the animal receive attention in the liturgical directions for this sacrifice.

12. The "pleasing aroma" arises out of the smoke that is made by all the burning ingredients that are on the altar—animal flesh, flour, oil, and incense. While God is portraying Himself in an anthropomorphic fashion, as if He used a human sense of smell, the phrase functions as a statement of acceptance of the offering. His favor toward the one who believes in Him, and who diligently obeys His instructions for Divine Service, constitute the offering's acceptance rather than anything that has to do with the offering itself.

13. The "pleasing aroma" motif occurs quite often in the New Testament. Paul lifts up Christ as the perfect, unblemished sacrifice who is not only the completely pleasing aroma offered to God the Father for the forgiveness of our sins but who also turns the unbounded favor of the Lord toward us. In response to our reception of this grace from Christ through the Holy Spirit, our life of faith and good works for the sake of our neighbor constitute the pleasant-smelling sacrifice that has set aside the ritual one that was prescribed in the Old Testament.

14. The prohibition against consuming blood goes back to the very moment when animals were given for food. For Noah and his family, along with all the animals that disembarked from the ark, God handed down the reason why blood is off limits: the life is in the blood. The blood of the one, perfect sacrifice—Jesus Christ, our Savior—will truly give life that lasts forever. In Leviticus 3, the fat of the animal is included in the prohibition for a similar reason: the animal's fat holds a tremendous source of energy. Israelites ate very little meat in their diet over a year, and they were to be markedly different from the pagans who ate fat and blood precisely to partake of the life and energy of the animals that they worshiped.

15. In the New Testament, all ceremonial requirements were removed, while the moral Law (the Ten Commandments) remained binding. Everything that once was prohibited is now made a matter of Christian free-

dom. While the apostles who met in Acts 15 clearly intended to remove the requirement of circumcision because certain Judaizers insisted on it, they agreed to keep a few voluntary restrictions for the sake of weak believers who would need to be catechized patiently in the freedom of the Gospel. In our day, we have similar opportunities to bear with those who, because of their sensitivities, need a bit of patient guidance. For instance, many churches have people who are aware of the freedom to drink alcoholic beverages at their social functions (in moderation, of course), but they still hold back from serving them for various reasons, but also lovingly to be mindful of the weakness of others.

Day 4 • Leviticus 4; Numbers 29:31–34, 38

16. The blood of the sin offering is allowed inside the tent of meeting when it is the priest who commits the unintentional sin. He is the one authorized to enter this nearer presence of God, and if the priest is soiled with sin, then he cannot perform his all-important vocation for the benefit of all. He still cannot enter the Most Holy Place at this time because only the high priest is allowed there, and that's only once a year on the Day of Atonement. The blood makes atonement that extends to the entire sacrifice by being sprinkled before the veil and dabbed on the golden incense altar. The rest is taken back outside to the bronze altar of burnt offering in the courtyard and the ash heap outside the camp.

17. The ash heap receives all parts of a sacrificed animal that are not meant to be on the altar of burnt offering. Those who handle them and burn them become unclean. These processes are outside the camp because the camp is the location of God's holy people, who are purified by the public sacrifices offered for them by the priests. The ash heap, where the by-products of sin offerings are continually burning, is an image that is used to help describe punishment in hell (see Revelation 9:2; 14:10; and 19:20).

18. The elders act on behalf of the whole congregation of Israel in much the same way as the male heads of households offer sacrifices for their own families. In the case of a sin offering for all the people, every one of the elders would lay their hands on the bull that was going to be offered in sacrifice for the sake of the nation. Once the priest brought the blood into the Holy Place to make atonement, then the announcement of full forgiveness would be proclaimed to the people. By the Lord's own promise, they all are forgiven with that one offering.

19. Depending on the vocation of the person who committed the unintentional sin, the sin offering varies in size and comparative value. Priests and other leaders have larger animals than do common Israelite citizens. The leaders also must offer male animal sacrifices, while the others are commanded to bring a female. The ordinary people are also given the opportunity, if finances demand, to offer birds or even flour as a sin offering substitute. This is not a difference in people's importance before God but a difference in order as they relate to one another in their callings. The forgiveness is still the same for all, as it is distributed by the priest's act of making atonement.

20. A sin offering is required on each day of the Feast of Booths, as the passage from Numbers details. No particular sin is confessed; thus one could draw a comparison to our modern-day liturgical practice of speaking together a general confession of sins at the beginning of the Divine Service. Sin and its forgiveness remain the emphasis, even in the joyful atmosphere of a festival to the Lord.

Day 5 • Leviticus 5

21. The order to speak in testimony to a matter was very important in the civic life of the Israelite community. Since God was supreme ruler over His people, His laws required full cooperation of all in enforcing them. In his commentary on Leviticus, Dr. John Kleinig notes, "This was an important device for the administration of justice in a close-knit society without a police force, where people often kept silent to cover up for their kinsfolk or to get back at their enemies" (*Leviticus*, p. 119). This importance places this sin of omission in the same category as ritual uncleanness by contact with something unclean.

22. Flour is allowed as a substitute sin offering, but it then does not serve the same purpose as the flour used in the grain offering (Leviticus 2). The latter is a joyful, free act of thanksgiving, so therefore the oil and incense are included to reflect that spiritual attitude. A sin offering omits those extra ingredients, and the black smoke that it creates in the fire does not include the distinctive odor they give but rather matches the sin for which it is meant to atone. The offering is also meant to be placed on top of all the other earlier sacrifices that have already been placed on the altar of burnt offering.

23. The guilt offering includes a repayment of something owed to God, either for breaching His holy liturgical rubrics or committing deceit or robbery. Christ offered His soul for this kind of offering on behalf of all believers, as Isaiah 53 portrays His saving acts as our Suffering Servant. By faith in Him, our debt to our Creator has been paid in full.

24. Answers may vary. Encourage discussion, if possible, beyond the mere reaction to death and blood, and look for insights that people may have into the entire system of sacrifices and offerings centered on the tabernacle and altar. Would you in this situation be more eager for the promised coming of Christ?

25. Ritual is sometimes described merely as repetition of familiar routines and rote incantations. If that means mindless (and faithless) mouthing of words apart from understanding and meaning, then of course that kind of ritual would be detrimental. But ritual also gives us words for our use in bringing our requests to God, and it assists us in hearing His forgiving and loving message to us. People who are trained from an early age to be independent and creative in self-expression may have a more difficult time seeing the value in a ritual that helps define and shape a community (or Christian congregation) and bring people together as one body with many members.

Priestly Ministry

Leviticus 6–10; Numbers 3–4; 12; 15; 18–19; Deuteronomy 12–13

Preparing for the Session

Central Focus

The priests stood between God and men in a complex sacrificial system that was meant to prepare for the coming of Christ. Now that our Savior has completed His saving mission through His death, resurrection, and ascension, we Christians are privileged to identify ourselves as royal priests, offering our spiritual sacrifices by faith in Him.

Objectives

That participants, led by the Holy Spirit working through God's Word, will

1. gain an insight into the Aaronic priesthood and the role of the Levites;
2. appreciate the value of a divinely appointed intermediary priest; and
3. relate the priestly duties described here to our roles today as royal priests of God.

For the Small-Group Leader

Small-Group Discussion Helps

Day 1 • Leviticus 7; Numbers 3–4

1. The priests were given a portion from the grain offering, sin offering, guilt offering, and peace offering for them to eat, so long as these were offered by somebody else. These holy foods had to be consumed in the courtyard of the tabernacle. The burnt offering was not allowed to be consumed because it was intended to burn up completely on the altar; then the leftover ashes were taken away to the ash heap. If a priest offered any of the other offerings on his own behalf, he was not allowed to eat that sacrifice—it had to be burned up, that is, given entirely to the Lord.

2. The freewill offerings could be consumed on the day they were sacrificed (corresponding to Good Friday), or the day after, but by the third day (Easter Sunday), they had run their course and belonged completely to the Lord; they must be burned up. This helps us see that the Bible counts days using a consistent pattern. Of course, it should also be remembered that a new day was begun at sundown, given that the creation account in Genesis 1 repeats the phrase "and there was evening and there was morning."

3. While Moses and Aaron were still in Egypt, Aaron was chosen to be Moses' mouthpiece to speak to Pharaoh. This arrangement was made when Moses complained that he was unable to speak due to "uncircumcised" (i.e., fat or clumsy) lips (Exodus 6:30). Once the Israelites left Egypt and entered the wilderness on their way to the Promised Land, Aaron's role changed to become God's anointed priest, along with his sons, to serve before the Lord in the Divine Service.

4. Aaron was the first high priest; his sons would be in line to succeed him and function as the other priests who were granted access to the holy places in the regular course of administering the offerings before the Lord. No one could enter the tabernacle except when a sin offering was made, and no one but the high priest once a year could enter the Most Holy Place. The priests had specific directions already laid out for them, so they were considered more as public servants than leaders. The Levites were men from the same tribe as the priests, but were not of the direct family line of Aaron. They helped the priests and ate some of the food offerings, but they were not allowed near the holy places and vessels. The rest of the Israelites, represented by the male heads of households, could only bring their personal offering and kill it, if an animal is involved, but then the priest would perform the rest of the task. The common people were not allowed any more access to God's holiness than that. Men were appointed to serve in these worship functions because the Lord had other special vocations to give to the women of all Israelite tribes.

5. When Israel sets out on its journey, following God's presence in the pillar of cloud and fire, the holy vessels are covered in skins and cloth by the priests who already have been granted privilege to approach them. Then, when there is no more risk of seeing or touching the holy things, a specific division of the Levites, the sons of Kohath, are allowed to lift these items by their carrying

poles and walk with them, keeping themselves centrally located in the Israelite congregation even when on the move. Other Levite divisions are given the responsibility of carrying other items such as curtains and supporting rods, according to the directions laid out in Numbers 4.

Day 2 • Leviticus 6; 9; Numbers 18–19

6. While it is true in other places of the Old Testament that repetition serves as a form of emphasis or significance, here in Leviticus, the directions for the various offerings are given first from the perspective of the people who are to render the offerings, then from the perspective of the priests, concerning what they are to do with the offerings once they are brought forward. So instead of functioning merely as a summary, this section of the liturgical directions describes what the priests and Levites do once the other people have departed the altar area. Leviticus 7:38 also points out that the Lord gave these latter directions to Moses on Mount Sinai, whereas the former instructions were spoken "from the tent of meeting" (Leviticus 1:1).

7. The fire was kept burning as a testimony to the Lord's gracious presence with His people, and it demonstrates His willingness to accept their humble offerings of confession, thanks, and praise. This constant flame served as but a reflection of the pillar of fire that God Himself kept burning as Israel continued their years of wandering in the wilderness. Since the altar was in constant use for the various sacrifices on a daily basis, it simply made good practical sense that its fire should be constantly ready to receive the next burnt or other offering. Of course, when it came time to pack up and move, the fire was put out and the ashes dumped (Numbers 4:13).

8. The priests and Levites eat the food of the offerings that are brought before the Lord because they are the designated holy people. They are worthy to eat by God's grace, not by any works they have done. This is no "take out" meal for the priests and Levites, however—since the offerings are holy, the food that the servants eat from these offerings must be consumed in the courtyard in the presence of the Lord. God has designated this as part of their inheritance, since none of them were given their own land to possess as a tribe, as God gave to the other tribes.

9. The Levites had fewer privileges and holy duties than the priests did. They were set apart from the rest of Israel, but their work was to serve and remain "out of the spotlight," as it were. They were required to be subordinate to their relatives of a higher calling. A person who was naturally self-aggrandizing would have to take a huge dose of humility before he could be a faithful Levite. These men were most likely unassuming, attentive to detail, and hard-working. It would be helpful here to point out to students that these roles were not chosen by the individual, so regardless of a person's type of personality, he still had to heed God's Word above everything else and seek forgiveness if he transgressed the limits of his job description.

10. The priests of the New Testament are called upon to offer sacrifices, but these are spiritual in nature, as opposed to the physical offerings that were administered by Old Testament priests. Priesthood is by birth in both cases, but now that birth is given by water and the Holy Spirit in Baptism. Christians today, as "royal" (kingly) priests, are granted access to the Father, and through Christ, this access is even more direct than that the high priest had in Leviticus. Priests of both eras offer prayers to God on behalf of others, but the true, sole Mediator, whether we are talking about Old or New, always has been and always will be Jesus. The Old Testament priests were simply anticipating the point in created time when the Word would become flesh to be our Savior.

Day 3 • Leviticus 8:14–30; Deuteronomy 12–13

11. The blood of Abel cried out to God after Cain murdered him in the field. Because the field received Abel's blood, Cain could not farm the ground anymore and was made into a wanderer. After the flood, God protected human life by demanding the blood of the killer as payment for the blood of the victim. Blood speaks of the image of God in this important passage. In Exodus, blood was the first plague, and the protection from the final plague was offered through blood on the doorpost. When Ezekiel was given a charge to serve as a watchman, he was held personally responsible for the blood of the people, meaning not only their physical life, but especially their spiritual condition.

12. Blood is used throughout Leviticus, following the rule "The life of every creature is its blood" (Leviticus 17:14). The life of the animal stands in for the life of the one offering the animal. This exchange is important, because it is central to atonement and justification, the most direct references to Christ found in the Bible. Blood sets apart and declares something holy and de-

voted to the Lord and His covenant, just as it did on the first Passover.

13. When the priests were ordained in the area in front of the tent of meeting, blood was poured out on the altar, splashed on its sides, and dabbed with the finger on its four horns. Then the blood was applied to each priest's right ear, right thumb, and right big toe. After the blood was mixed with oil, it got sprinkled on the priest as he wore his vestments. This would remind the priest that he was set apart for his holy task, and the people watching the ordination ceremony would take to heart the requirements of the Lord that are necessary for the priest's redemption from sin.

14. The sacrifice of animals, as described here in Leviticus and elsewhere in Scripture, is always a response to a specific word and promise from God. Sin itself is a violent rift that separated us from God, and it took the violence of Calvary's cross to mend it. By a swift stroke to the throat to minimize suffering, believers took the lives of animals during Old Testament times in service to this greater message of salvation that would come to completion in the Christ of the New Testament. Their deaths were the farthest thing from senseless violence at the hands of a deranged abuser.

15. Answers may vary. It would be helpful to emphasize the central teaching of Scripture that is being highlighted by the shedding of blood: God's forgiveness is given to us freely in Christ. Often, Christianity is limited in people's minds as being about morality only, but that understanding robs the believer of the Gospel itself.

Day 4 • Leviticus 8:1–13; Numbers 15:37–41; skim Exodus 28; 39

16. Answers may vary. Students may point to the precious stones or gold appointments as particularly outstanding. For instance, the stones on the breastpiece and shoulder are engraved with the names of all the Israelite tribes. When the priest enters God's holy presence, he is reminded, as are the people, that he stands in for them, and that he is a type of the perfect mediator and sacrifice, Jesus Christ.

17. Vestments provided a cover-up for the quirks and individuality of the person who held the priestly office at a time when the holy things he handled deserved all the emphasis. They are meant to call all attention to the spiritual actions going on, and to direct attention away from the imperfect sinner who is doing them. This function of vestments also holds true for office holders in the New Testament Church. While vestments are designed to discourage the urge to "lord it over" the laypeople, the Lord's servant would do well to maintain an ongoing regimen of personal repentance in light of the vocation he holds in order to ensure that his position or its symbols are not misused for personal gain.

18. The saints in the vision of the Book of Revelation wear white robes as they hold palm branches in their hands. Vestments are not just a privilege of priests and clergy; all who believe have been washed white and clean of all sin and defilement in the blood of the Lamb, and their vestments are signs of this gracious, divine gift to them in body and soul. The former sacrifices and ceremonies of all times and places were preparing for this heavenly moment when the forgiveness of sins and purity given us from the Lord's hand will admit us as a redeemed, holy people to the glorious presence of the holy and righteous God, who sits on the judgment throne.

19. The item that God commanded all the Israelites to wear is a tassel on each corner of their garments. It was meant as a device to remind them of God's commandments and promises, keeping them from following other gods. They were to avoid anything that would attack their faith in the Lord who brought them out of Egypt—the great salvation event of the Old Testament.

20. Just as the white garments in the Book of Revelation give testimony to our common salvation in Christ, so Christ is our holy garment we put on at Baptism, covering our sins, as we are reminded in Galatians 3:27. We are granted the privilege of access to God's throne as we offer spiritual sacrifices of praise and prayer. The people we remember in prayer, just as the priest remembered the names of the tribes engraved on the stones, are the ones whose needs we bring before the Lord, confident that He will bless them according to His good will.

Day 5 • Leviticus 10; Numbers 12; 15

21. The first two sons of Aaron, Nadab and Abihu, changed the Lord's prescribed method for offering sacrifices. The term we are given in the Bible is that they offered up "unauthorized" or "strange" fire before the presence of the Lord. Since the transgression involved incense, the brothers may have done something that would have defiled the Holy Place inside the tabernacle. At any rate, they took matters into their own hands and

intentionally disobeyed God's express commandments concerning the tasks of their holy office. Nadab and Abihu were burned up themselves because of their sin.

22. King Saul impatiently offered up a burnt offering, thus stealing away the role of priest from Samuel. He reasoned that he needed the Lord's blessing before the military situation he was facing got any worse. Rather than heeding God's Word and placing his trust in the work of the appointed servant of the Word, Saul acted contrary to the Lord's command and lost his kingship to David as a result. Compared to the death of the priests who disobeyed (see previous question), Saul was granted a gracious reprieve. However, it doesn't look like he took advantage of the opportunity to repent.

23. In Peter's speech before the apostolic Jerusalem Council in Acts 15, he addresses the topic of what Christians should do with the requirements of Moses, especially circumcision, when it comes to welcoming converts from among the Gentiles. The burden, or yoke around the neck, was constituted by all the laws, statutes, and ceremonial directions that accompanied circumcision. If you impose one facet of the Old Testament ceremonial law, then you had better be ready to keep all of it perfectly. The Gospel, however, would grant freedom of conscience in these ceremonial matters, uphold the universality of the moral law, and, most of all, proclaim the Law's total fulfillment in Christ. Peter seems to say that by his time, the thought of keeping all of Moses' commands, as outlined in the Pentateuch, was considered impossible.

24. The priest and Levite in the story of the Good Samaritan pass by the victim, who had been beaten on the road and left for dead. Their liturgical duties required that they not touch a dead body, or else they would become unclean. While they made a hasty assumption that was meant to spare them the time it would take to be cleansed and eligible for service, they neglected the true opportunity to serve, which is the mercy that only the Lord's own sacrifice could give. This is why, in this story, the Good Samaritan is the character who depicts the saving work of Christ. While it isn't the main point of the parable, it points out that the Old Testament rites and ceremonies, with their demands for ritual cleansing, would soon come to an end giving preference to faith in Christ and love for neighbor.

25. God held the people, and especially the priests, responsible for any desecration of His name or His holy things in worship. The closeness of His presence was life and blessing to believers, but death to those who approached on their own terms and made a mockery of God, as was evidenced by the death of the two priests who offered "unauthorized fire" before the Lord. In the Lord's Supper in Corinth, now that the Lord was present in real human flesh, those who ate the Lord's Supper in an unworthy manner, that is, without proper examination and faith, were guilty of sinning against the true body and blood of the Lord. They did not receive a blessing but were punished, some with sickness or even death. The reality behind the ceremony, whether we are talking about sacrifices or the Sacrament of the Altar, is the holiness of God, the closeness of His presence in Christ.

Clean and Unclean

Leviticus 11–15; Numbers 5; 19; Deuteronomy 14; Luke 2

Preparing for the Session

Central Focus

Ancient biblical concepts such as clean and unclean are all but lost on our contemporary culture. Even to well-versed Christians, the distinctions can seem meaningless and arbitrary. This session will clarify what is going on with this incessant process of purification and shed a possibly unexpected light on our life of joyful repentance.

Objectives

That participants, led by the Holy Spirit working through God's Word, will

1. trace the various activities described in relation to the concepts of clean and unclean;
2. follow along as the process of ritual purification is delineated; and
3. discover the ultimate answer for removing the stain of sin through Christ.

For the Small-Group Leader

Small-Group Discussion Helps

Day 1 • Leviticus 11; Deuteronomy 14

1. The two features that assist God's people in figuring out which mammals are clean are chewing the cud and parting the hoof. Fish need to have fins and scales. Insects need to be able to hop. Various flying animals are listed that are unclean. Rodents and lizards are listed by specific type to identify them also as unclean. Hares and rock badgers are mentioned particularly only because by their observed mouth motions they appear to chew the cud. However, since they don't have the required cloven hoof, they do not meet both criteria.

2. Aaron is included with Moses at this point in Leviticus because he was made high priest. He is taking over some responsibilities in these matters, since the priests will continue these duties long after Moses is gone. Flipping through the book, one can see this address to both Moses and Aaron occurs a few more times, but Moses remains the primary recipient of the Lord's instructions.

3. This section of the chapter departs from the domain of the sanctuary and courtyard and describes the unclean animals that will turn up in the Israelites' homes. This emphasizes that the liturgical purity of the Divine Service extends also to everyday life. Here is where they are going to find a dead mouse or come across a lizard. This is a reminder for people to be mindful of God's gracious activity at all times. Anything that will get in the way of His dealing with men in worship will also obstruct His activity in other places.

4. The Divine Service that we observe on Sundays can influence our everyday life in our vocation. We could offer up in our personal prayers the specific petitions that were prayed when we were gathered together with fellow believers. The readings, hymns, and sermon can provide the substance of our meditation and prayer throughout the week. Just as the Israelites were instructed to pass their rituals down to their children, so we could teach our next generations what is going on in the worship service or discuss a particular Bible story. Even our baths and showers can be utilized in a spiritual function to put us in mind of our Baptism, and every meal can remind us of the great feast of Christ's body and blood that is given us in the Sacrament of the Altar.

5. The distinctions between clean and unclean were an important way that God's people thought constantly about their faith relationship to their Lord. Staying away from unclean things would ensure that a person was still granted access to God's gracious presence in order to offer a gift or sin offering. Those who did not care whether they were ritually defiled betrayed that their faith inside was sick or lacking altogether. In our day, we do not have unclean items or foods, but our anger against someone who has hurt us can fester and obstruct God's good gifts and forgiveness to us. Our favorite habitual sins or pleasures can be made into idols toward which we direct our devotion instead of to the Lord. Thinking of these things as "unclean" could be helpful in taking a serious approach toward indwelling sin and how it affects us.

Day 2 • Leviticus 12; Luke 2:22–39

6. The purification process following the birth of a child required first a period of ritual uncleanness. For the birth of boys, the mother was unclean for a week; for girls, she remained unclean for two weeks. Following this initial period, she waited another thirty-three or sixty-six days. Then, when the forty (or eighty) days were done, she (note that it is not the head of the family acting for her) would offer two sacrifices for her purification. A substitute offering was allowed for mothers who could not afford a lamb for the burnt offering.

7. Answers may vary. One may expect an offering of thanksgiving, or a prayer for health and safety of the child. The connection to sin and its curse does not always come naturally to the human mind upon the birth of a child. Of course, this rite does not imply that it would be considered a sin for a mother to give birth. It is certainly true that our society today has very different rituals with very different emphases whenever this occasion occurs.

8. Because her firstborn was a son, Mary would offer the sacrifice to the Lord on His behalf at the same time she fulfilled the ritual for her own purification. Giving birth to a male child meant that she would be allowed into the temple courts when Jesus was forty days old. The Gospel notes that they gave the substitute offering of two birds, rather than a lamb and a bird. By giving this lowly sacrifice, indicative of poverty, they testify to our Lord's great love to come among us in humility to be our servant Savior, the true Lamb of God.

9. Blood is significant in this description of uncleanness and purification following childbirth. The mother's time of uncleanness is compared to those times when she would undergo menstruation, the flow of blood. The unclean period comes to an end when a male child is circumcised (blood is shed) on the eighth day; two weeks for the birth of a girl—possibly because a daughter would carry on the divine gift and ability to bear children. The mother's purification is specifically tied to her flow of blood, not because the blood itself carries any special divine power but because the Lord has set it apart as an indicator of His gift of life.

10. Separation from the community occurs upon the birth of her child. Her uncleanness keeps her and the baby away from interaction with others for an initial period of time. After her male child is circumcised (or after two weeks if the child is a girl), this strict separation is eased up a little and she begins to make her transition back into everyday living; however, she is not yet included in the liturgical rituals of the Holy Place, nor allowed to touch the holy things or eat the holy food. Once this transitional phase is complete, then the mother brings forward the offerings for her purification, and she will be declared clean and eligible for worship, as well as for all of normal daily life. Attention to this ritual would impress upon the woman her role to bear seed in her vocation, especially to carry on the Genesis 3 promise that a woman would bear the one Seed, Jesus, who would crush Satan's head.

Day 3 • Leviticus 13; Numbers 5

11. There are approximately eighteen different skin diseases that fall under the broad category of "leprosy" or "leprous disease" in Leviticus 13. Then, toward the end of the chapter, there are a few varieties of infection that would need to be examined in garments. The people with the specified maladies would be brought to the priest because he is the representative of God and the one responsible for applying His definitions of clean and unclean. Presumably, this was done at the Holy Place in the midst of the camp, where the priests perform their other works of service.

12. As the priest examines the different symptoms on each person's skin, he looks for a white spot. In some instances, the hair dies and loses its dark color, and so white hair inside an infected area indicates an unclean disease. A few serious cases look deeper than the skin, so they require the cleansing that is described in subsequent chapters. Ask the class for any surprising discoveries. One could mention as an example verses 12–13, when the whiteness from the chronic leprous disease covers the whole body, head to foot, and even though the person was pronounced unclean previously (v. 11), now he would be considered clean, so long as there is no raw flesh exposed.

13. Jesus commanded the ten lepers to walk to the priests and receive the ceremonial pronouncement that was given to them since the time of Moses and Aaron. He also knew, of course, that He would heal them as they went, so that if they finally make it to the temple (Luke doesn't say specifically whether the nine others actually got there or not; we may assume that they did), then they would demonstrate before God's presence their ceremonial cleanness and receive a favorable verdict from the priests. This obedient act would serve to demonstrate their faith in God that trusts His Word.

14. The Samaritan in Jesus' encounter with the lepers would not be allowed before the priests because of his status as an outsider to God's holy people. Even if he were clean from his disease, the man would not be able to enter the Lord's presence located in the temple. Yet, the Samaritan enters the Lord's presence when he turns back and falls down before Jesus, who is the Son of God standing right there before him! As Jesus points out at the end of this narrative, it is the faith of the Samaritan leper that saves him.

15. Even an inanimate object like a garment needed to be cleansed from disease. The same great care had to be taken as though it had infected someone's skin. Uncleanness could be transferred, so anything with which a person might come into contact would need a professional judgment from an Aaronic priest. Working from the idea of transferring uncleanness and putting it into positive terms, the New Testament passages that address clothing ourselves with Christ bring to mind how He purifies us and makes us clean from sin and our old self, wrapping us in His righteousness as with a (clean) garment. These verses also bring out the identity that is drawn between Baptism and putting on Christ, complete with the fruits that this relationship bears in the Christian's life.

Day 4 • Leviticus 14

16. The first round of ritual cleansing from leprous disease involves two wild (ESV: "live") birds. One is killed, and its blood is mixed with water. The other bird is dipped in the watery blood mixture, which is then sprinkled on the person, and then it is let go back into the wild. The next group of sacrifices happens on the eighth day, after the person is allowed back into the camp (yet he must still remain outside his tent). The animals sacrificed then include two male lambs and a ewe lamb. Added to these is a grain offering of flour and some oil for anointing.

17. The blood of the first bird stains the live one to highlight the cleansing significance of blood, along with the clear idea that one life was substituted for the other. The stained bird is let go so it can join the other birds in its flock, just as the person who had once been separated from his family and community by his uncleanness may then be restored to his group and vocation, thanks to his cleansing at the hands of the priest. This particular bird ceremony is used for the various leprous diseases and for cleansing a house that has been infected.

18. When a leper is cleansed with the blood of a male lamb, the blood is applied to his right earlobe, the thumb of his right hand, and the big toe of his right foot. This is similar to what happens when a priest is ordained. The blood sanctifies the ear for hearing God's Holy Word, his hand to touch holy things, and his feet to walk in sacred space. For the priest, the blood of ordination is not considered an atonement. Both are anointed on the head with oil. What is different is that the ordination blood came from a ram, which is a little older specimen, and the oil is added on top of the blood in those same three spots for the leper before he is anointed on the head with the rest of the oil.

19. Answers may vary. Discuss how priorities can change when a sudden crisis like this takes place. Perhaps it would be similar to when a disaster strikes a house and only a few possessions are really worth saving. Pets, pictures, heirlooms, and other treasured items would most likely top the list of things that one would not want pronounced unclean and untouchable.

20. Jesus doesn't appear to be concerned about whether a house is unclean before He enters it. Levi the tax collector is blessed to share a meal with Jesus; that communicates to him a bond of acceptance and fellowship with the Lord—he is now one of Christ's chosen disciples. When Jesus visits the house of Zacchaeus, He announces that, upon the sinner's repentance, "Salvation has come to this [formerly unclean] house" (Luke 19:9). The Magi entered the house inhabited by the child Jesus and, even though they were unclean Gentiles, His blessing was granted to them as they presented the Lord with their gifts. Christians may request a pastor to bless their home and family, because a blessing takes the Word of God and dedicates to Him someone or something that was at one time in the common or evil realm.

Day 5 • Leviticus 15; Numbers 19

21. Leviticus 15 lists several ways that uncleanness arises from a normal or abnormal bodily discharge. The person's bed and anything he sits on would be unclean; no one could touch him, or else the uncleanness would transfer. Spittle, saddles, earthenware vessels, and sexual contact are all included as means of spreading that which would keep someone away from holy things.

22. For those who needed to be cleansed from the uncleanness of a bodily discharge, the sacrifice always involved two turtledoves or two pigeons. At other times (e.g., Leviticus 5:7–9), these two birds are offered as a

less-costly alternative sin offering for a poor person. There is no such option given here.

23. Several places in Leviticus and Numbers state that the person may be declared clean following a ritual bath that would occur in the evening. This recalls the Bible's reckoning of the start of a new day at sundown on the evening before. A new day is then greeted with a new start on behalf of a person who, in confident faith, fulfilled the requisite sacrifice or other ritual.

24. Someone who has suffered personal violence, especially of a sexual nature, can easily feel defiled and unclean. An act that would solidify love under the blessing and bond of marriage becomes a most hideous intrusion that cannot be easily put out of mind, especially if it came at the hands of someone who at one time was a trusted individual. Many victims, in fact, often feel that the injury is permanent, and they feel so ashamed that they become convinced that God wants nothing to do with them. These unclean feelings can be usefully addressed head-on through Scripture and especially through evangelical counsel from a pastor or another trusted Christian.

25. When a woman with a discharge of blood—which certainly was a matter of constant uncleanness—touches Jesus' garment, He immediately perceives His own healing power transferring to her in order to remove her ailment. It is not explicitly stated, but it appears that Christ is absorbing her sin and shame while He makes her well. The sinful woman in Luke 7 similarly approaches Jesus without presumption of deserving His mercy, and demonstrates her love in response to His purifying forgiveness, though Simon the Pharisee doubts Jesus as a prophet only because it seems to him that Jesus can't tell that she is unclean. In fact, He is much more than a prophet because He can actually remove the uncleanness! The Good Samaritan stands for Jesus as He cared for us in our need, including our unclean spiritual status due to sin. By way of contrast, the Law (depicted by a priest and Levite) was incapable of stopping to help us.

Atonement

Leviticus 16–17; 21; 23; Numbers 29; Matthew 6; Hebrews; 1 John 2

Preparing for the Session

Central Focus

Atonement lies at the heart of Israelite worship during the wilderness wanderings, just as much as it does for us Christians in the twenty-first century. A final, full, and universal atonement was achieved for us by the Son of God, Jesus Christ, our Lord. As the Book of Hebrews attests, He is the focus of this significant ancient ritual event, as well as that of our Divine Service today.

Objectives

That participants, led by the Holy Spirit working through God's Word, will

1. identify the Old Testament concept of atonement and the ceremonial Day of Atonement;
2. link this important ritual to its fulfillment in the cross of Jesus Christ; and
3. incorporate these emphases into a fuller spiritual practice of repentance and faith.

For the Small-Group Leader

Small-Group Discussion Helps

Day 1 • Leviticus 16; 23:23–32; Numbers 29:7–11

1. A bull and a goat are sacrificed as a sin offering on the Day of Atonement. Numbers 29:7–11 adds a burnt offering and grain offering above and beyond this. Two goats are presented for the casting of lots, an action that decides which one is sacrificed to the Lord and which one is to live and be sent out into the wilderness as a scapegoat (or "Azazel").

2. The Day of Atonement ceremonies are meant as a time for confession and absolution of all sin (including outright rebellion against God) for the entire people through the priest as their spokesman. The Lord's holiness is accessed by the high priest, who then comes back into the realm of the laypeople to distribute that holiness to them in His stead. The sin offerings that take place every other day are meant for unintentional sins only and are not judged as sufficient for all kinds of sin.

3. Some possible synonyms, depending on the English translation, include *expiation, redeem, sacrifice, fragrant offering, satisfaction,* and *substitution.* Most of these Bible passages are speaking of the work of Christ for the forgiveness and salvation of the entire world. Believers receive the benefit of atonement for their sins, and if a person rejects atonement, then that person's sins are held against him or her.

4. The ritual of the scapegoat is yet another instance that illustrates and communicates the forgiveness and eradication of sin. Multiple forms of God's grace highlight His manifold mercy. Just like the other animals that are killed on other occasions, the Azazel goat receives the laying on of hands to transfer sins upon its head. The priest lays hands and confesses sins on behalf of the whole nation. This is the main difference from those sacrifices that people offer on behalf of themselves. In this ceremony, blood atonement is not emphasized, as it is in the sacrifices, but another form of Gospel proclamation is employed.

5. The Day of Atonement is a good place to start when explaining how the other rituals make sense. The ceremony's correspondence to Christ is very clear. It relates to the central truth of the Gospel. Discussion should focus on how everything in the Old Testament has a relationship to Christ, and how the atonement is Christ's chief work of salvation.

Day 2 • Leviticus 17:1–9

6. The tabernacle is God's self-designed and self-chosen holy place to interact with His people for their spiritual good. He makes the rules because it is His grace that allows sinners to come before Him for forgiveness and praise. Every day, many animals gave their lives in the sacrificial system. Lest the people get desensitized to this routine slaughter, the Lord held the shed blood against the people if they forgot the all-important truth that the sacrifices need to conform to His direction. This was not meant to exasperate the people and bind them unnecessarily. Rather, it extols faith as the highest requirement.

7. Uzzah was killed for handling the ark improperly as it was being moved by cart from the village of Kiriath-jearim. The oxen pulling the cart stumbled, and Uzzah put out his hand to touch the ark, evidently to steady it or keep it from falling. No indication is given as to why the ark was pulled by cart rather than carried by its poles as directed in Exodus and Numbers. King David responded to the outbreak of the Lord's anger by leaving the ark alone for a while in a Levite's home. When it was treated with genuine respect, then the Lord brought blessing, and not another burst of anger.

8. While the permanent tabernacle was being built, Moses set up a temporary tent of meeting that was quite some distance from the camp. The pillar was at the tent and the Lord spoke to Moses there until the specified tent and courtyard were completed. Then it occupied the central position that it kept throughout the rest of their wilderness wandering. The Levites were given a camp around the tabernacle to give them access to their assigned holy tasks. The eleven other tribes (Joseph was split up according to his sons Ephraim and Manasseh) were situated in groups of three camps, located at the four sides of the court. Once the nation arrived in the land of their inheritance, a specific location would be set aside in one of the tribal territories to set up the tabernacle and court. A temple would not appear in Jerusalem until over four hundred years later.

9. The Lord has already revealed Himself in the Ten Commandments as a "jealous God" (Exodus 20:5). He cannot abide His chosen and redeemed children to commit spiritual adultery with any other gods. Goat demons and their mythical antics were popular among other surrounding nations, so there would be a constant temptation to include them in their worship practice. These other gods, as spoken of later in Scripture, are not gods in fact, but actually demons. There is no common ground between the true God and demons, and to disregard this important distinction would be a serious affront to the Lord's holiness.

10. The ark of the covenant in 1 Samuel 4–5 was brought out to the field of battle in the hopes that it would prove to be a good-luck charm. The dramatic turn in the story is that the Philistines, who heard the confident battle cry of the Israelites, nevertheless strengthened themselves for battle and defeated God's people, because the Lord no longer found any genuine faith in the Israelites' hearts. The ark had become just another god to the Israelites, so ironically they believed the same way that the Philistines did. The news of the ark's capture brought death to Eli, as Samuel's message of punishment had promised. The Philistines were allowed to capture it only because the ark *per se* is not endowed with power, but God's will went with it. His power certainly made itself known to the unbelievers, who suffered various ailments and whose idol was humiliated before it.

Day 3 • Leviticus 21

11. The high priest not only has charge of all the sacrifices on the Day of Atonement, but he also is charged on this one day only with the task of taking the blood of the sin offering into the Most Holy Place, where he must sprinkle it on the ark of the covenant and incense altar. He needs to wash and put on special linen garments for this activity, and wash again when he completes the task. No other time shall he get this close to the central location of God's presence on earth. He still cannot approach without an atonement made for himself. He must be unblemished and not be ceremonially unclean, as defined by any of the various requirements that priests must meet in order to handle holy things.

12. Priests may be cleansed from uncleanness like anyone else, but due to their holy tasks, they still must meet certain standards that are higher than the rest of the Israelites. The priests are given an exception due to the need they may have to bury close blood relatives, but not the high priest. A priest's own wife would have to have her family take responsibility for her funeral rites so that he could remain faithful to his holy duties, which come higher than family in this instance.

13. The priests stand as representatives of the people to God, and they stand in for God in His blessing back to the people. Only the unblemished can stand in God's holy place. The descendants of Aaron who are blemished are still allowed to have holy food brought to them outside the innermost holy area to eat. This makes it clear that they are not being punished for being disabled or "imperfect."

14. Potential priests may not have blemishes or deformities, or else they cannot come near to God's holy presence and touch the holy things. This would be essential to their role as atonement-offering makers. The priest stands in for the people in order to point their faith squarely to Christ, who was spiritually and physically unblemished for our sake.

15. Christians are royal priests in the New Testament Church, and they have an access to God through Christ that is even closer than the priests and high priests had

in the Old Testament. In place of mere showbread, they eat Christ, the Bread of Life. They must love Jesus above all others, including their own families, if it ever comes to a choice between the two. They have even more stringent commandments concerning divorce; they are called to a life of holiness; they share in the sanctified status of Christ through their suffering; and they gain ultimate access to the real, heavenly throne of God in their prayers.

Day 4 • Hebrews 2; 5; 7–10; 1 John 2

16. Jesus is the Son of God who clothed Himself in our human flesh. Similarly, the high priest, on the Day of Atonement, would put on special clothes to approach the Most Holy Place and perform the propitiation for the sins of the people. Jesus was tempted in every way, as we are, yet remained without sin (Hebrews 4:15). He died in real human flesh, shedding real blood, which because of the union of His divine and human natures, is the blood of God that makes a once-for-all sacrifice that puts away sin totally (Hebrews 9:25–26). Rising from the dead in human flesh makes Him the "firstfruits of those who have fallen asleep" (1 Corinthians 15:20). Because Christ performed His complete task of atonement and salvation in our human flesh, we have the assurance that He acted as a perfect substitute for our sake.

17. The priestly order of Melchizedek is prior to that of Levi, since Abraham paid tithes to Melchizedek while Levi "was still in the loins of his ancestor" (Hebrews 7:10). Melchizedek appeared "without father or mother or genealogy, having neither beginning of days nor end of life, but resembling the Son of God he continues a priest forever" (Hebrews 7:3). This historical priority and eternal status makes Melchizedek compare to the Levitical priesthood as an object compares to its shadow. This corresponds to how Christ Himself compares to the high priest as the latter is described in his role during the Day of Atonement ritual.

18. Christ is not a Levitical priest; for one thing, He is descended from the tribe of Judah and not Levi (Hebrews 7:14). He belongs to the order of Melchizedek because He, too, is without beginning or end. His sacrifice is not after the manner of the directions given in Leviticus because (a) it is His own blood that He presents to the Father; (b) He enters not an earthly tent, but the very heavens themselves; (c) the curtain is not made of animal skins, but His own flesh; (d) He ministers in a better, permanent covenant; and (e) He offers the sacrifice not yearly for a limited number of people but once for all.

19. We offer our prayers as sacrifices that Christ presents as High Priest in our stead before the Father's throne of grace. This confirms our status as royal priests, baptized into an eternal, heavenly kingdom and purified by His all-availing sacrifice. Our good works of service to our neighbors combine with our prayers for them as holy and priestly works that our God performs through us. We do not act on our own; we are agents of our heavenly Father, just as we serve as a go-between in prayer for our neighbors.

20. The Word of God in 1 John 2:2 is quite clear about the universal atonement that was secured in the death of Christ as a propitiation. Similarly, John 3:16 could be invoked because the word "world" encompasses all people. When someone observes that not everyone goes to heaven, the appropriate response is that it's not a fault of Christ's atonement. Instead, the truth remains that many will reject the salvation that has been fully earned for them. One does not need to solve this theological question with the unbiblical answer that it is people's choice to believe in Jesus. The parable of the banquet invitations and wedding garments (Matthew 22:1–14) is a helpful tool in moving the conversation from popular philosophical opinions about God to what He actually says about Himself in His Word.

Day 5 • Leviticus 16:29–34; Matthew 6:16–18

21. Fasting is commanded of the whole nation of Israel for the entire Day of Atonement. Leviticus 16:29 says, "You shall afflict yourselves," so that God's people would demonstrate their repentance over their sin by denying themselves food, drink, pleasure, and work as a solemn Sabbath rest. Doing so would help them to see what great lengths it must take to remove their guilt and iniquity. The hunger they would feel would be a poignant reminder of the curse that sin has brought on them and on the world.

22. Fasting is accompanied by sackcloth, ashes, dust on one's head, and mourning over a loss or death, among other things. These examples reveal times when fasting served as an individual's or group's reaction to dismaying events. The Ninevites fasted in response to Jonah's preaching of impending judgment, even though they were not yet assured of the Lord's forgiveness. Note how

the entire city fasted once the king made the proclamation and set an example, as though he were "head of the household," to use the catechism's phrase. The fasting on the Day of Atonement is different because it is liturgically mandated as a yearly occurrence. It includes a joyful response to the forgiveness that was achieved through faith in the Christ to come, as expressed in dutiful obedience to the ritual legislation.

23. The practice of fasting that Isaiah criticizes in chapter 58 is one that trusts in the human activity of fasting to guarantee a positive result just because it is done for God. Faith is absent in this attitude toward good works in general, as the Lord points out in verses 3–4. Fasting without faith in the Lord's forgiveness of sins is useless, as Isaiah himself says (64:6); our "righteous deeds are like a polluted garment."

24. Our Lord, in the Sermon on the Mount, leaves the practice of fasting open to the freedom of the Gospel; however, He does assume that many believers will at least consider it for their own personal discipline, given His words, "And *when* you fast . . ." His point on fasting in Matthew 6 is centered on the requirement of faith and the importance of refraining from the practice as a means of self-aggrandizement. Our fasting, whether we choose to do it or not, will be "rewarded" in secret from our heavenly Father, not because we are so good at refraining from food, but because our heavenly Father is pleased with us by virtue of our Baptism into Christ.

25. Answers may vary. Keep in mind that fasting should not be looked upon as a dieting regimen. Also, if it is specifically dangerous to your medical condition, then you shouldn't put your health at undue risk. Especially, it is important to keep in mind that one's conscience should not be bound in it. Fasting is to remain a voluntary expression of individual faith, even if a whole congregation or church body recommends it. Abstaining from pleasures, candy, television, and such for a time can be considered fasting when properly bound together with true faith and God's Word.

Holiness

Leviticus 17–22; Numbers 6; Deuteronomy 7; 9; 17–18; 21; 24–25

Preparing for the Session

Central Focus

God's holiness is what sets Him apart from all the false gods and distinguishes Him from the creation that fully depends on Him. Thankfully, however, He chooses not to use His holiness as a weapon to distance us from His mercy, but rather grants the power of His holy name to save us, to establish a close relationship with us, and to answer our prayers.

Objectives

That participants, led by the Holy Spirit working through God's Word, will

1. survey the multiple ways that God's holiness is confessed concretely in the Torah;
2. understand why holiness is an essential attribute for both God and Church; and
3. articulate the prophetic office of Christ, using Moses as a pattern.

For the Small-Group Leader

Small-Group Discussion Helps

Day 1 • Leviticus 17:10–16; Deuteronomy 7:1–16; 21:1–9

1. Blood is the life of an animal, and it is set aside to make atonement. It is not meant to be eaten, since God's system is incompatible with the pagan religions that say a person would derive a certain benefit from eating blood. God will cut off pagans from His holy people and set His face against them.

2. When God sets His face against a faithless transgressor, it indicates His wrath and judgment. In Numbers 6, God provides for the priest to say, "The LORD make His face to shine upon you" (v. 25), which means blessing and forgiveness for the penitent faithful. The Lord's shining face of blessing is coupled with His name so that His identity is bestowed on them for their peace and protection. Believers may then call on Him in thanksgiving and offer prayers for help.

3. The command to destroy completely or devote to destruction is intended only for Israel in their holy task at this time in their history. No one has this directive from the Lord anymore because its purpose has been fulfilled. Similar to Jesus' telling the rich young man to sell everything, or God telling Abraham to kill his son, these examples are not written in Scripture in order to be general rules. Devoting a nation to God upon His specific orders by destroying them is to carry out divine wrath against their corporate sin. These devoted nations are "holy"; they are subject to His just judgment. They belong to Him, and nothing is to be spared, just as burnt offerings must be entirely incinerated. No one has part of anything that has been totally devoted to the Lord.

4. Answers may vary. If a killer is unknown, family of the victim do not feel much comfort in their grief, but the ceremony would at least acknowledge the crime, a heifer would lose its life on behalf of the offender, and the town elders would give their solemn word that they did not do it or see it. Just like unsolved murders now, those who are closely related to the victim would receive patience and comfort from God's Word of promise that His ultimate judgment will be swift and final.

5. Jewish and Gentile believers found themselves together in many places once they were baptized Christians. Different customs and freedoms were bound to conflict in these early years. For a brief time, even in communities completely convinced of the true freedom of the Gospel, certain prohibitions were difficult to give up, since these were ingrained in the Jewish culture. So, out of deference for some weak consciences, and only for an interim period, not eating blood would be *requested*, not *commanded*, by the apostolic council in Acts 15 to fulfill the law of Christian love for one another.

Day 2 • Leviticus 18; Deuteronomy 24–25

6. The Lord goes into detail concerning certain sexual practices because the Israelites had probably seen some of these forbidden activities taking place in Egypt, and they were going to see them in Canaan, where they were headed. He wanted them not to follow the immoral practices of these enemy nations but rather to remain holy to the Lord and to confess His name in what they do once they settle in the Promised Land.

7. The land promised to the Israelites was a gift from beginning to end. They would not earn it by their efforts; God was the owner; they were to be the stewards. Their condition for living in the land of their inheritance is to follow all the statutes, laws, and ceremonies, or else the very land itself will cough them up like a stomach reacting violently to poison or something else that it deems repulsive. This is what is happening to the Canaanites and all the other nations whom Israel will drive out.

8. The less-than-ideal arrangement of multiple wives is depicted in the Old Testament with grief, animosity, and some form or another of childlessness. Sarah mistreated Hagar, Hagar pushed back; Hannah was doubly loved, yet also despised and ridiculed for her unfruitful womb; Jacob was tossed around from one wife to the other, and even treated as a commodity (Genesis 30:15), but he was also shared with the women servants in order to produce sons. Despite these departures, God's people still end up receiving the fulfillment of His promises.

9. Matthew 19:8 quotes Jesus as saying that because of the Israelites' "hardness of heart," Moses allowed divorce on the grounds of "indecency" (Deuteronomy 24:1). The first husband may not take his divorced wife back, because she was "defiled"; this is a ceremonial term and therefore this case is not applicable in the New Testament setting. Marital infidelity that cannot be resolved with repentance and reconciliation may unfortunately lead to divorce, recognizing that in those difficult situations, the marriage has been killed off already.

10. Both ceremonial procedures concern widows without a male heir. Both involve removing a sandal from one's foot—in Deuteronomy, it is done in the context of an insult against a man who neglected his duty; in Ruth, it is the custom to document publicly the transfer of rights of a redeemer from the first in succession to the next. The commentary in *The Lutheran Study Bible* (p. 429) notes that the symbolism in handing the sandal to Boaz was to give him "the right to step onto the property" and claim it, along with the right to marry Ruth.

Day 3 • Leviticus 19; Numbers 6

11. "I am the Lord" or "I am the Lord your God" serves as a refrain to tie all of God's commands and prohibitions to His exclusive claim to His people as His possession. They represent Him to the world, so by their actions Israel, eagerly expecting the coming Christ, confesses their faith in the one true God for the benefit of all the other nations.

12. In addition to keeping the Sabbaths and performing proper offerings to the Lord, the people of God were to refrain from stealing (Seventh Commandment), not deal falsely (Seventh, Ninth, and Tenth), leave some fruits and grains in one's fields and vineyards for the hungry and traveling (Fifth), do no injustice in court or slander (Eighth), and not swear falsely (Second and Eighth).

13. The common bond between these seemingly unrelated pronouncements are the mixture of two things that God wanted to remain distinct, just as the people were to remain distinct from all other peoples. Different kinds of cattle are not to breed, fields are not to be planted with two different kinds of seed (presumably at the same time, not one after another), and people should not wear clothing made from two different kinds of fabric. An exception to the latter rule is made when God Himself directs the priests' holy garments to be made of linen and other colored yarn woven together.

14. The Nazirite vow was, above the general promises of all Israelites, to be devoted to the Lord. Your students may see that food requirements and avoidance of the dead and diseased involve some temporal benefits; allow them to offer more suggestions. The extra strictures and offerings described in Numbers 6 serve to set the man or woman apart to the Lord as holy. This was to declare publicly one's faith, not to earn justification. See Romans 3:20–25. (See also Article XXVII of the Apology of the Augsburg Confession.) Christ is the ultimate holy one dedicated to His mission, not for Himself, but for the sake of all people. He did not break His vow to be committed to the world's salvation.

15. Samson lost his strength upon the cutting of his hair, not because it possessed any inherent strength on its own, but because he broke his vow to the Lord and forfeited divine strength, which he had taken for granted. The hair was a key sign that Samson was dedicated as a Nazirite. Not all Nazirites had superhuman strength, to be sure, but his vow would be part and parcel of Samson's role as Israel's judge and deliverer.

Day 4 • Leviticus 20; 22; Deuteronomy 9:1–12; 17:1–7

16. The worship of the pagan god Molech involved more than just a prohibited mixture of Canaanite religion with the worship of the one true God; it also threatened the Israelite family. Children were sacrificed to this false deity in hopes of increasing fertility and material wealth. Such a breach of faith, aside from being outright murder, would also be equal to utter rejection of the Lord who is both Creator and Redeemer.

17. Moses hearkens back to the early days of Israel's

wandering and points out to the new generation of Hebrews that God's grace was with them and their fathers from the beginning. Everything that happened by His provident hand had occurred "without any merit or worthiness" in them, to quote the Small Catechism. They did not earn their status as God's favorite nation by being great and numerous, nor was it because their righteousness was stellar among all the other peoples.

18. The Israelites did not earn the right to kick out the nations from the Promised Land and take possession of it. Rather, the nations there had deserved the Lord's wrath, and so He would evict the former tenants and bring in others who would live in a plentiful land by God's good pleasure. Genesis 15 notes that the Amorites will increase in their iniquity until the time comes when the Lord, through Israel, the holy children of Abraham, would render them their due punishment. If God's people themselves break away from Him, He will destroy them in a similar retribution (see Deuteronomy 30:17–18).

19. The requirement for an unblemished animal for sacrifice helps preserve holiness by leading the Israelites to identify the perfect sacrifice who will come, namely Christ. Anyone who worships the created things as idols, instead of the Creator of all things, should be investigated and stoned if found guilty. As serious as this charge is, it must require two witnesses, and this was the very requirement that the Jewish leaders were finding difficult to meet at first when they were fishing for a legal excuse to execute Jesus (Matthew 26:59–60).

20. Holiness is bestowed on the Christian Church also solely by God's grace. He calls His Church to Himself through the preaching of His Word and the administration of the Sacraments in accord with that Word. When Christians repent and remain grounded in the Word, they are constantly prepared to give an answer to anyone who may ask for the hope they have in Christ (1 Peter 3:15). Holiness is to be distributed to all who hear the Word and believe. It is not now meant anymore to be kept away from those who do not yet have faith.

Day 5 • Deuteronomy 18:15–22

21. Moses spoke to the Lord face-to-face, and he was the direct link to God Himself. The messianic Prophet is like Moses in that He speaks God's Word directly, yet He also supersedes Moses in that He is God Himself living in human flesh. Moses once came down off the mountain and put on a veil so that he would not overwhelm the rest of the people by the brightness of his face. Jesus would be hidden in His lowly form of a servant (Philippians 2:6–7) so that the people could listen to Him, be healed, and believe in the forgiveness of sins that He will pay for with His own precious blood.

22. If the words that the prophet speaks do not come true, then that person is a fraud, and not the promised Messiah. If God did not command it, then the prophet is not to speak it. Jesus was completely obedient and subject to His heavenly Father in passing on the Word that He was to speak and teach for the benefit of all who would listen to Him. He is the Blessed One who comes in the name of the Lord, just as the Jerusalem crowds had acclaimed Him on Palm Sunday.

23. The respected Pharisee Gamaliel echoed the test that Moses gave for proving whether a prophet is telling God's true Word. He advised leaving Peter and the other apostles alone and wagered that if the Christian faith were really illegitimate, as the council assumed, then it would fail because it merely was of man. If it was of God, then there would be no way to stop anything about it, because then His mighty hand would be behind the effort. "You might even be found opposing God!" (Acts 5:39).

24. The Christians in Berea heard Paul and Silas preach the Good News and then searched the Scriptures (the Old Testament) every day "to see if these things were so" (Acts 17:11). Their eagerness to receive the Lord's Word and to apply the rest of the Bible to what Christ had already done prompted honorable mention from the writer of Acts, Luke. If the Bereans examined those Scriptures that were written in the time of the wilderness wanderings, perhaps the tabernacle, the sacrifices and priestly worship rules would be for them clear references to Christ, along with the rescue of Israel from Egypt pointing directly to our Savior's death and resurrection for our eternal salvation from slavery to sin.

25. The Galatians were instructed by the apostle Paul to pronounce an eternal curse ("anathema") against anyone who proclaimed a different Gospel. No one was exempt from this on the basis of their person alone—Paul even included himself and an angel straight out of heaven among *anyone* who might even try to alter the truth of free salvation by grace through faith in Christ alone. Even though another Gospel is really no Gospel at all, the distortion is appealing to people's self-centered Old Adam, who does not want the gift of salvation and desires to worship the self as God.

Festivals

Leviticus 23–25; Deuteronomy 15–16

Preparing for the Session

Central Focus

The idea of having a Church Year originally came from God. Israel was commanded to observe days and seasons in their ceremonial law so that the Lord's mighty works of salvation would be declared in its fullness. Though today we are free from these commandments, we would do well to continue commemorating the boundless mercy of our heavenly Father that has been revealed to us in His Son.

Objectives

That participants, led by the Holy Spirit working through God's Word, will

1. gain a better grasp of the main holidays and observances covered in these books;
2. compare these holy days with celebrations within the Christian tradition; and
3. grow in their own spiritual preparation as it is conditioned by the Church Year.

For the Small-Group Leader

Small-Group Discussion Helps

Day 1 • Leviticus 23:1–3; 25:1–7; Deuteronomy 15

1. The Sabbath, the seventh day, is a weekly day of "solemn rest" when God's people do not work but set aside the day for worship. There are seven other holidays during the year in which work is to cease: the first and last days of Unleavened Bread, the closing day of the Feast of Weeks, the Feast of Trumpets, the Day of Atonement, and the first and last days of the Feast of Booths. Only the Day of Atonement, however, follows the exact pattern of the Sabbath in prohibiting all work. The other festivals call for no "ordinary work," which is work in connection with the peoples' means of livelihood.

2. The greater rest indicated by the Sabbath observance is a confident faith in the completed work of salvation achieved for us by Christ's death and resurrection. This rest is denied to those who refuse to believe and whose hardened hearts drive them to works of disobedience. The baptized believe the good news that came to them, and they are united in one faith with those who preach that sharp two-edged sword of the Word of God.

3. The analogy of the six days of creation is important in the context of Leviticus 23:3, as well as in the Third Commandment, as given in Exodus 20:11. In either place, there is no hint of a merely symbolic connection to creation. The week is seven days long precisely because that is how long it took the Lord to make the world and then declare a day of rest. Those who insist on the theory of evolution are better off avoiding the Bible altogether for the sake of honesty and consistency.

4. God blesses works of mercy on the Sabbath, and Jesus proved this through His healing miracles that drew the anger of the Jewish leaders against Him. Instead, He is the promised Messiah, the Son of God who has come to bring release from the hold that sin and its curse have on the world. His ministry, which leads up to Calvary's cross, demonstrates His lordship over the Sabbath (Mark 2:28).

5. The Sabbath received its complete fulfillment when our Lord rested in the tomb on the Sabbath following His death. His close followers also rested (Luke 23:56) to obey the commandment, but a new day would dawn with His resurrection on the first day of the week (Luke 24:1; John 20:1). Paul would not only teach in the synagogues on the Sabbath but would also "break bread," that is, worship Jesus in the Lord's Supper with fellow Christians on Sunday, the first day of the week (Acts 20:7). By the time Revelation was written, this anniversary day of Christ's resurrection became known as "the Lord's day" (1:10). The Sabbath, having done its work, slowly gave place to the new day of rest and worship.

Day 2 • Leviticus 23:4–8; Deuteronomy 16:1–8

6. Now that the tabernacle had been set up in the middle of the Israelite camp, a food offering was incorporated into the festivities for Passover. Even at the very

beginning, the Feast of Unleavened Bread was meant to last seven days. The lamb's blood would not be spattered on the doorposts at any further celebrations of the Passover, because that ceremony was specifically tied to the final plague in Egypt, the Angel of Death.

7. The Passover lamb and the Feast of Unleavened Bread recalled for God's people the memory of His magnificent act of salvation in Egypt. But remembrance involved more than just a mental exercise or object lesson. Through this yearly meal, the Israelites took part themselves in what the Lord had done for their forefathers. Whatever happened to the people in 1446 BC happens continually in later years and centuries by means of celebrating the festival in faith in any time or place.

8. Passover is included in Gospel accounts of Jesus, especially in John, because He is the true lamb of sacrifice. Going back to when He was twelve years old, He was in His Father's house during His family's annual Passover pilgrimage, amazing the teachers. When John notes that the Passover was "at hand," he is tying the present event (e.g., the feeding of the five thousand in John 6) to our Lord's sacrifice and the benefit that it brings to us in faith. Christians who read or hear these accounts then see how Christ is connected to the festivals that they now observe.

9. The Lord's Supper was completely instituted once Jesus and His disciples drank "the cup, after supper" (1 Corinthians 11:25). It does not include the sacrifice of a lamb because Jesus, the real thing, has taken the place of the shadow. We do not include the bitter herbs (Numbers 9:11) because we now rejoice in the full salvation that Christ achieved, to the extent that our former bondage and bitter suffering will no longer be remembered. The Passover was a week-long observance once a year, but among the earliest Christians, the Lord's Supper took place on the first day of the week, every week. This is because the Lord's Supper isn't exclusively based on Passover, but it also comes out of Christ's table fellowship with His disciples and hearers, especially during the forty days following His resurrection.

10. A familiarity with what goes on in the Passover is helpful to understand what Paul is writing to the Corinthians about removing the leaven in their midst (1 Corinthians 5). He points to Christ, the sacrificed Passover lamb, and the new observance of the festival with hearts purified by a sincere and true faith. Good Friday is the new Day of Atonement because, at the death of Jesus, the temple curtain was torn in two, revealing access to God not through a veil but through His own flesh (Hebrews 10:20). Colossians teaches us that the Christian faith did not start in a vacuum, and all of the Israelite festivals were "a shadow of the things to come, but the substance belongs to Christ" (2:17).

Day 3 • Leviticus 23:9–22; Deuteronomy 16:9–12

11. *Firstfruits* is the sheaf of grain that is the first to be harvested from the field, and it is set aside to be waved as an offering before the presence of the Lord. The whole harvest belongs to the Lord, and this initial offering on the part of the Israelites recognizes the number one priority of giving thanks and recognition to God for giving them everything. All of His gifts are holy, and the firstfruits ceremony releases the remainder of the harvest for His people's personal use as His stewards.

12. A steward is someone who takes care of something that really belongs to someone else. Dr. Kleinig (*Leviticus*, p. 506) depicts the Israelites' offering of firstfruits as their "rent" that they gave back to God, who was the true owner of the land and all the crops. In a similar way, we should think of our stewardship not as a mere portion that we owe to the Lord, but rather remember that everything belongs to Him and once we make an offering from the first and best, then He gives us back the rest of what we have, authorizing us, if you will, to use His possessions with His blessing. Our firstfruits are "rendered" to Him in thankfulness "for all His benefits to me" (Psalm 116:12).

13. Before the Feast of Weeks, the grain offering is a sheaf of barley waved by the priest before the Lord. Seven weeks are then counted off to reach the day of the Feast, when the priest waves two loaves of leavened bread. Yeast is allowed in the bread for this offering because it is not going to be burned on the altar. The sacrifice that is offered with the firstfruits is one male lamb as a burnt offering, and some flour mixed with oil and wine is to be burned as a food offering with a pleasing aroma. In early Judaism, the next Feast was named Pentecost because it took place on the fiftieth day after the wave offering. Seven lambs are offered (perhaps standing for each of the seven weeks), and a bull and two rams are presented as a burnt offering. Then there is a sin offering of a male goat and a peace offering of two male yearling lambs; these are offered along with the bread, not to be burned but to be consumed by the priests in the Holy Place. The first grain is barley, and

by the time Pentecost arrives in the late spring, the key bread ingredient is the first wheat of the season.

14. On the same day that firstfruits would have been offered in the presence of the Lord by the priest on behalf of God's people, Jesus Christ, the Son of God, rose from the dead to secure everlasting life for the entire world. The forgiveness of our sins and our hope of heaven, both for ourselves and for those who have already fallen asleep in death, rely upon the resurrection of our Lord. He is, therefore, the true firstfruits, having been offered to God the Father on the cross by laying down His life, only then to take it up again on the third day. He is the first to rise from the dead, meaning we will follow His lead and rise also to eternal life on Judgment Day.

15. Pentecost is closely tied to harvest because Israel was an agrarian community. All aspects of life, including the growing seasons and animal husbandry, were dedicated to worshiping the Lord. The earliest results of the harvest were presented to the Lord in the hope of a plentiful future harvest. The era of the Church that began at that first Christian Pentecost featured a worldwide harvest of believing souls, whom God appointed in Christ unto salvation by grace. In Acts 2, many people from various far-off nations were already gathered in Jerusalem to celebrate the Jewish festival; they ended up hearing in their own languages the wonderful works of God, as told by those believers who were given the Spirit's gift at Pentecost. These first Christian believers then spread the Gospel in their respective countries. The apostles soon followed close behind them, establishing churches wherever the Gospel was being preached. The harvest that was begun then will not be complete until our Lord comes again on the Last Day for judgment.

Day 4 • Leviticus 23:23–25, 33–44; Deuteronomy 16:13–17

16. The seventh month of the Israelite calendar would begin at the new moon with the Feast of Trumpets. This month was the "Sabbath" month, and it included the Day of Atonement, the important festival in which all of the peoples' sins would be paid for in blood and forgiven. The Feast of Booths would then take place soon after the Day of Atonement.

17. Rams' horns are specifically mentioned in Exodus 19, when the Lord appeared to Moses and all of Israel at Mount Sinai. The trumpet blast signaled His presence and called everyone's attention to what He was about to command them. Rams' horns were also used to sound a warning of an attack, as the watchman was ordered to do in Ezekiel. Joshua had the priests sound a long blast on rams' horns when the Lord was about to destroy the walls of Jericho and hand the city over to his army. The silver bugles (or "cornets" as other versions translate it) are described in Numbers 10, and they have much the same sacred and military use. They also signaled the beginning of festivals and the new moon. Trumpets were especially employed to announce the new reign of kings, as was done for Solomon when he ascended to the throne as co-regent with his father David.

18. The people of Israel lived in booths that were pitched around the Lord's tabernacle. These were meant to give temporary shelter to the pilgrims while the festival observance was going on. This was a yearly reminder to these people and to their descendants after them that the Lord had rescued them from slavery in Egypt and, while they were in transition to their inherited land in Canaan, they had had to live in tents out in the wilderness. More than merely re-enacting the past event, they were reminded that they were only "passing through," that their true home awaited them elsewhere. We Christians could take to heart that we are only "strangers and exiles on the earth" (Hebrews 11:13). We are a holy people, set apart from the unbelievers, and awaiting our true home in heaven, where Jesus has gone before us to prepare a place (John 14:2).

19. Similarities between the Feast of Booths and the Muslim pilgrimage: a visit to the holy place is required, the male head of household is especially commanded to attend, people dwell in temporary shelters, offerings are required, it is a seven-day observance, there is animal sacrifice.

Differences: the Muslim requirement is once in a lifetime, but Israel was commanded to attend the Feast of Booths each year; Muslims change clothing to wear all white; Israel has trumpets, but Islam has spoken voice chanting; the priest performs the ritual within the holy space for the Israelites, but all Muslims who make their pilgrimage circle around and bow before the Kaaba in Mecca.

There is no equivalent in Islam to the Hebrew Day of Atonement because Allah does not give forgiveness of sins by means of the death of a Savior. Muslims observe a time of sacrifice (known as Eid al-Adha) out of obedience to Allah's command, but not to obtain atonement.

20. John introduces His Gospel with Christ, the Word who became flesh and "dwelt among us." This is God

the Son inhabiting human flesh as a tabernacle. The Lord who led Israel by a pillar of cloud and fire would teach them with His own human mouth, eat and drink with His people, heal their sick and perform miracles by the power of His divine Word, and suffer to the point of death on the cross for our salvation. When Jesus offered up His own life as the sacrifice for the sin of the whole world, the need for the temple and the whole atonement ritual came to an end. So the temple curtain was torn by God "from top to bottom" (Matthew 27:51) to make it clear that Christ's flesh and blood would grant all believers access to the Father in Him. The difference between our Lord's human body and the temporary booths would be that for Him, flesh and blood is not a temporary dwelling. His body is now glorified in His resurrection, is seated at the right hand of the Father in holy majesty, and is distributed with His blood in the Lord's Supper.

Day 5 • Leviticus 25

21. The land was set aside for the Lord in the Sabbath year when the people refrained from cultivating it, much like the Sabbath day every week was dedicated to the Lord when the people refrained from work on that day. Their fields were to lie fallow until the following year, and whatever grew of itself could be used for food. God promised that He would give enough of a harvest yield during the sixth year to last them through the Sabbath year and up to the harvest of the next year (Leviticus 25:21).

22. The jubilee year is proclaimed in addition to the seven Sabbath years leading up to it. Again, no cultivation of crops shall be done, but additionally there is to be the release of servants ("proclaim liberty throughout the land"; Leviticus 25:10) and all lands that were bought and sold during the previous fifty years were to be given back to the original owners.

23. God commanded the jubilee to assert that He was the one and only owner of property and His people. Just as He had set Adam in the Garden of Eden in order to "work it and keep it" (Genesis 2:15), the Lord had distributed the Promised Land as an inheritance to the tribes of Israel so that they would take care of it as though they were renting from Him. Even when property changed hands, it was only passing from one caretaker to another. The jubilee was all about giving a fresh start and marking a once-in-a-lifetime celebration of the Lord's providence.

24. Property would not transfer at the jubilee if it was a house located within the walls of a city, because it was not reckoned with the land surrounding it. If a house inside a walled city was not bought back within a year of its sale, then that house belonged to the owner in perpetuity. It was the land that constituted the divinely bestowed inheritance. Also, if a Levite were to sell a house in one of their cities, he would be allowed at any time to buy it back up to the year of jubilee, at which time it too would be released back to the original owner. The Levites are an exceptional case in all of these rules because they were given only cities and their immediately surrounding lands, instead of an entire region of their own in the Promised Land. Because of their special service in the holy places, "the LORD is their inheritance" (Deuteronomy 18:2).

25. The Christian jubilee is not a release of property or freedom from servitude in the physical sense. Christ our Lord does grant us freedom from sin and its bondage (which Paul described aptly in Romans 7), and that freedom is given to us through the truth of His Word. Our slavery was paid for through the redemption that cost our Lord His suffering and death. There is now no condemnation for us, because we have been delivered from this body of death, and in our Baptism we were granted an everlasting inheritance of faith. Our relationship to others has changed too, because in Christ there is no longer slave nor free, and those who once were slaves now share with their former superiors one Master, who is in heaven.

By the "Numbers"

Numbers 1–2; 16–17; 20–26; 31; Deuteronomy 31; 34; 2 Kings 18

Preparing for the Session

Central Focus

Having already consulted various parts of the Book of Numbers, we will now delve into material exclusive to this book. These events signal a crucial turn in the wilderness wanderings, and will set the stage for what will continue after the Pentateuch comes to a close. Numbers is a book that you definitely do not want to skip!

Objectives

That participants, led by the Holy Spirit working through God's Word, will

1. recognize census and numerology in their contexts as they relate to proclamation;
2. be able to sort through the timeline of events that comprise the wanderings; and
3. be more comfortable with using material from these books in personal study.

For the Small-Group Leader

Small-Group Discussion Helps

Day 1 • Numbers 1–2; 26

1. The first census is taken immediately after the Israelites gather in front of Mount Sinai. Its purpose is to collect an offering, or "atonement money," to pay for the services of the tent of meeting that is being built. The second one is designed to count the fighting men and prepare Israel for their holy battles that will secure for them their inheritance in the Promised Land. The final census counts the new generation of wanderers because they will be the ones to inhabit the land that God is about to give them.

2. The Levites are included neither among the fighting men nor among those who would settle in their own territory once the Israelites arrived in the Promised Land. Their whole tribe is set apart to serve the Lord in His holy space—before the tent of meeting. They exclusively handle the holy items when the camp moves from one place to another. The Levites are still counted separately, but instead of their males being counted at twenty years and older, they are counted at one month of age and older. The Levites stand before the Lord in place of the firstborn from all of Israel, because they are the priestly tribe.

3. The tribe of Levi is taken away, but the tribe of Joseph is divided among his two sons, Ephraim and Manasseh, and they are treated as though they are two tribes. Manasseh is further divided in half when the people begin to settle in the Holy Land—some on the east side of the Jordan River, and others with an inheritance of land with the other tribes on the west side. The number twelve is prominent in the Bible, speaking of God's holy people of Israel, and also of the twelve apostles in the New Testament. The number three stands for God the Holy Trinity, and four stands for the four corners or directions of the world, so the two multiplied together yield the Church, the sum of all believers.

4. The Israelite camps surround the four sides of the tent of meeting that is in the center, three on each side. Levi is stationed at the tent itself. The three are sometimes grouped together based on their matriarchal roots among Jacob's wives. The tabernacle and its holy furniture would travel at the center of the group, just as it is central when their camp is set up. Jacob arranged his family in similar groups, separated among the four mothers, Leah, Bilhah, Zilpah, and Rachel. When they settle in the Promised Land, these clusters of tribes would in some cases keep in close proximity to one another.

5. Judah is in the lead whenever the Israelites move, as Jacob had predicted in his words of blessing recorded at the end of Genesis. From him and his son Perez, whose mother was Tamar, his widowed daughter-in-law, would come King David and the royal line ("scepter"; Genesis 49:10) that would lead eventually to Christ. In contrast to Reuben, the firstborn, Judah offered himself to Jacob as a substitute in case Benjamin were harmed during the return trip to Egypt (Genesis 43:8–9), an act also fulfilled by the Messiah, who would be descended from his family line. He is our substitute to the heavenly Father, the one sent to redeem the world.

Day 2 • Numbers 16–17

6. Korah and his associates rebelled against Moses and Aaron, falsely claiming that these two men, ordinary as they were, exercised authority over the people of Israel because they considered themselves better and more spiritual than those whom they led. But he did point out something that is certainly true: "All in the congregation are holy, every one of them, and the LORD is among them" (16:3). But Korah and the 250 others left out the important truth that God Himself had placed these leaders in their position, and they were actually serving the people, not trying to "lord it over them" (Matthew 20:25). The dissenters wanted the privileges of leadership and of the priesthood for themselves, and they rejected God's plan of grace toward His people.

7. Moses and Aaron, humanly speaking at least, must have had every temptation to treat this conflict as a personal attack. Instead, they turned the matter over to the Lord, who is the One who placed them in ministry. At one time, Moses would have readily agreed that he, for all his faults, was unworthy of the position he was given (Exodus 4:13), but now Moses was confident in God's call and the power of His Word. Aaron, also confident in his divine calling, stood with his brother, and even when the Lord unleashed His anger upon the grumbling people, he bravely ran into the path of deadly wrath and made atonement for the very ones who resented him.

8. Aaron's staff was one of twelve that were placed in the tent of meeting before the Lord's presence in the Most Holy Place. The staffs represented the leaders of each tribe, and Aaron was chief over the tribe of Levi. God miraculously made Aaron's staff blossom and produce almonds to demonstrate Aaron's appointment to his holy vocation among the holy people, and to "make an end of their grumblings against Me" (Numbers 17:10). This staff was included for some time inside the ark of the covenant (Hebrews 9:4) as a constant witness to the ministry established by the Lord, not men, in order to administer His Means of Grace and salvation in Christ.

9. In a way even greater than Old Testament Israel, all baptized Christians are God's holy people. In fact, they are all members of a royal priesthood, according to 1 Peter 2:9. Christian laypeople are obligated to pray, because through Baptism they have been given the privilege of access to the Lord's presence that formerly was only granted to the Levitical priesthood. The Third Commandment lays out the responsibility for Christians not to despise preaching and the Word, but rather gladly to hear and learn it. The Christian pastor is responsible for laboring in the Word and doctrine, to care for the people the Lord has given him through preaching and the sacraments. Each role is meant to assist, complement, and support the other, thereby building up the Church as the Body of Christ (1 Corinthians 12:27).

10. Answers may vary. Some helpful Scriptures include 1 Corinthians 12; Ephesians 6; Philippians 2 and 4; Matthew 18; Hebrews 13; 1 John 4. Encourage the study of the procedure in Matthew 18:15–20, since personal sins often threaten the peace in a congregation. It is also appropriate to pray for your pastor, even at a time when you are disagreeing with him. God is able to sort it out and bring repentance where He knows that it is needed. It takes a great gift of faith to set the desires of one's sinful nature aside in a time of conflict and make room for the good fruit of the Holy Spirit. Discuss other suggestions from the group for trusted resources that would be helpful for congregational peace and reconciliation.

Day 3 • Numbers 20; Deuteronomy 31; 34

11. Numbers 20:2–13 records the second time that the Israelites in the wilderness grumbled against Moses and Aaron over the lack of water. They resented that God had led them out of Egypt, again forgetting their hard labor over which they cried to the Lord to save them. In total disregard for the Lord's promise of a good land in their near future, they provoked Moses to treat them as "rebels." In anger, Moses struck the rock with his staff, in disobedience to God's command.

12. The first time the people complained over the lack of water was shortly after they entered the wilderness and were camped at Rephidim, the place they occupied before moving on to the foot of Mount Sinai. Even with the exodus, the Red Sea incident, and the beginning of the miraculous gift of manna, Israel was not satisfied and doubted God's ability to take care of them. Now, in Numbers 20, their new generation renews the grumbling. They themselves had not seen God's mighty acts that are recorded in Exodus, but they clearly expressed the same doubts and complaints as their forebears.

13. Joshua will take over Moses' role of leadership, but he will not talk to the Lord face-to-face, the way Moses did. This helps the people look forward to Christ, who is like Moses, and even greater than Moses in that He will be God Himself in human flesh. As for Joshua, he

will instead consult with the high priest, who will be the designated messenger of God to Joshua. This exalts the Lord as sole leader of His people, whose glory will be given to no man. Now that He, through Moses and Aaron, has set up the priestly ministry as His Means of Grace to His people, God will operate through that means to lead His people through Joshua.

14. The ancient ceremony of laying on of hands is a signal that a specific Word of God or transfer of blessing is focused on the designated person. The hands would have been laid on the candidate's head as the chief part, as compared to the rest of the body (compare with the ceremony of laying hands on the head of the goat on the Day of Atonement [Leviticus 16:20–22] and Christ as the Head of the Church [Ephesians 5:23]). This remains as a symbolic gesture to this day, as it is used in the Christian Church for ordination, installation of church workers and volunteers, confirmation, and especially in the giving of private absolution to a penitent sinner. However, the power is not in the ceremony itself but rather in God's Word and His blessing that is attached to the liturgical action.

15. Moses was forbidden to enter the Promised Land as a direct consequence of his disobedient act at Meribah of Kadesh. Scripture uses the example of Moses to teach us the insufficiency of the Law to bring us forgiveness and eternal life. On the contrary, the Law makes us conscious of our sin and drives us to Christ for forgiveness in the Gospel. He is the source of saving grace and truth, and He sets us free from the law of sin and death, which would otherwise have prevented us from entering eternal life in heaven.

Day 4 • Numbers 21; 2 Kings 18:1–8

16. The Israelites complained again about the lack of food and water. God had commanded them not to fight against the nation of Edom or take their land from them. And when Edom refused even to grant them passage through the land, they were resigned to altering their course and go around that country. So Numbers 21:4 notes their impatience toward traveling back toward the Red Sea (this time, most likely, it is the Gulf of Aqaba). This impatience prompts the Lord to send fiery serpents to convict His people of their sin against Him.

17. Moses was instructed to make a bronze serpent and put it up on a pole. The Lord granted His Word of promise that anyone who was bitten by a real serpent and looked up to the bronze replica would live. Moses' serpent was not in itself a source of healing power, nor is it, interestingly enough, a "carved image" (Exodus 20:4). Instead, it is a sign of God's grace, because it is faith that makes the believer well (Mark 5:34).

18. Jesus was lifted up on the cross, just as "Moses lifted up the serpent in the wilderness" (John 3:14). Faith in Christ grants a believer eternal life and averts eternal condemnation. When Jesus died on the cross, He took away the stinging bite of sin and death. This story from Israel's time in the wilderness is a good context for one of the most well-known verses of the Bible, as it holds a promise of forgiveness not for those who prove themselves worthy but for sinners who fall to temptation and are beset with weakness, just like Nicodemus and the Israelites who lived many generations before him.

19. King Hezekiah had to destroy Moses' bronze serpent because it had become an object of worship, completely dissociated from its original use as a pointer to God's Word. It took nearly seven hundred years in this case, but any liturgical ceremony needs to be changed if it is employed in a way that contradicts the Gospel, for that would certainly cause irreparable spiritual harm, rather than good. (See Article X of either the Epitome or Solid Declaration of the Formula of Concord.)

20. We look up to Christ in the same way the children of Israel looked up to Moses' serpent. We are every day afflicted by our sin and the effects of sin's curse upon us. In the preaching of the Law, we are threatened by death and damnation. But in Christ, we have no mere example of how we are to follow the Law better, for that would put salvation out of our reach and, worse yet, it would nullify the blessed effect of our Lord's death and resurrection for us. While we look to Christ alone for forgiveness, trusting in the unconditional Gospel, we can then trust also in His gift of new birth in Baptism to lead us along the narrow path of sanctification and good works befitting a Christian.

Day 5 • Numbers 21–25; 31

21. The Israelite armies engage in battle with the noteworthy kings Sihon and Og while they are still east of the Jordan River. Sihon's realm is immediately to the north of Edom and Moab, while Og's domain is farther north in Bashan. Moses is still the peoples' leader, and the lands of these Amorite kings will be given to members of specific tribes to occupy after the rest of Israel conquers the Promised Land, west of the Jordan.

22. God promised the land to Abraham hundreds of years before, even while Amorites and other nations were occupying it. But in Genesis 15:16, the Lord noted that eventually His time of patience would expire concerning this faithless people, and their iniquity would reach full measure by the time Abraham's descendants defeat them. God commanded Israel to devote them to complete destruction as a necessary fulfillment of His just wrath.

23. Balak, king of Moab, called upon the prophet Balaam to curse the people of Israel. Balaam is evidently well-known for his effective divination practices, and Balak does not want the same fate that other kings, such as Sihon and Og, had received. So he sent the fees for divination along with a delegation that issued Balaam his request. He was so insistent that the second time around he even increased his offer and increased the number and honorable rank of his messengers.

24. The Lord forbade Balaam to curse Israel, because they were blessed. The Bible often uses the passive voice ("they are blessed") to refer to God's action (really, "God has blessed them"). Balak misunderstood the source of Balaam's ability to curse and bless, because it resided in the Lord, not in his own person. Balaam could be paid all the money in the world, yet "could not go beyond the command of the LORD my God to do less or more" (22:18). When he went with Balak's envoys, God sent the Angel of the Lord to stand in his way. At first, only the donkey could see the angel, and it turned to avoid death. When Balaam beat the donkey in order to keep going ahead, the Lord gave the donkey the ability to speak sense to him and finally then opened Balaam's eyes to see for himself.

25. The Angel of the Lord was sent as a spokesman for God, yet He was also addressed and even worshiped as God. He was the pre-incarnate ("before coming in flesh") Jesus Christ, the Son of God. Balaam admitted that he was standing in the presence of the Lord Himself, even though it was only after his eyes were allowed to see who it was. He had a track record of weakness, since previously he had shopped around for other sources of spiritual power (Numbers 24:1). Some other scriptural accounts of people witnessing the Angel of the Lord include Abraham as he is about to sacrifice Isaac, Moses and the burning bush, and God's announcement to Samson's parents about his birth and future role as judge of Israel. These other incidents were not examples of a time when God threatened death, so a closer similarity to Balaam's experience—even though the specific term "angel of the LORD" is not used—would be a story such as what happened to Moses on his way back to Egypt in Exodus 4:24–26.

Planning to Settle

Leviticus 26–27; Numbers 13; 32–36; Deuteronomy 1–4; 9–11; 19–34

Preparing for the Session

Central Focus

Turning our attention to the Book of Deuteronomy, we recount the forty years of wandering in the desert as they come to an end. Here the law is restated, past events are rehearsed, and the groundwork is laid for the future of God's people. By the time Moses says his good-bye and Joshua summons his courage to take over, we will have a good idea ourselves of our Lord's Torah instruction and how we may apply it faithfully in our walk with Christ as we journey to the future, heavenly promised land.

Objectives

That participants, led by the Holy Spirit working through God's Word, will

1. recall the Israelite tribes who did not settle in the Promised Land itself, and why;
2. find the promised land in all its details fulfilled in Jesus Christ; and
3. shine brightly as a blessing and witness of the true faith to our neighbor.

For the Small-Group Leader

Small-Group Discussion Helps

Day 1 • Numbers 13; 32; Deuteronomy 3

1. The descendants of Reuben and Gad wanted Moses to grant them the land that had belonged to the Amorite kings Sihon and Og. This would mean that they would possess no land in the Promised Land, west of the Jordan River in Canaan. Because they had a large amount of flocks and herds, they wanted to use the pasture land there for their animals and the cities of the defeated enemies for themselves. Initially, they had asked for Moses not to have them cross over the Jordan at all (Numbers 32:5).

2. Moses responded harshly to the people of Reuben and Gad because of their request not to go on with the other Israelites across the Jordan River. He was led to believe that these two tribes out of twelve would break away, and God's people would have to conquer the land of Canaan with a significantly smaller army. This would also cause a palpable decrease in morale among the ten other tribes, very similar to what the report of the spies did forty years previous to this. At that time, most of Israel was struck with fear and did not listen to the positive report of Joshua and Caleb, so they were punished with forty years of wandering in the desert. A similar punishment was threatened in Numbers 32:15, because if these tribes were to refuse to fight west of the Jordan, then not only would they be letting their relatives down, but they would also be disobeying the Lord.

3. If these tribes wanted to settle in conquered lands east of the Jordan River, then they had to agree to let their fighting men cross over with the rest of their relatives, once a place was secured for their animals and their people who would not be fighting in battle. The enemies in Canaan had to be defeated and the conquered lands assigned to all the other tribes as their inheritance before the men of Reuben, Gad, and the half-tribe of Manasseh would be allowed to return to their homes. Manasseh was divided in half because a certain portion of them captured eastern lands in a successful military mission, so Moses granted them the spoils that they had earned. The other half of Manasseh would eventually possess land in Canaan, west of the Jordan River.

4. The men of Reuben, Gad, and the half-tribe of Manasseh kept their word that they had promised to Moses before his death. They finished all the battles that were necessary for the rest of the tribes to gain their own allotments of land. When they were on their way back to their own homes, they built the altar of Witness, not to replace the true altar at Shiloh in Israel proper (which is what their relatives mistakenly thought they were doing), but to remind the future generations living on both sides of the Jordan that the eastern tribes needed to sacrifice at God's holy sanctuary, and the western tribes needed to allow them to come over to fulfill this duty.

5. Answers may vary. Vows are not required, but instead are completely a matter of Gospel freedom. Even so, however, vows still need to be taken seriously if one chooses to bind oneself to a promise before the Lord. If someone breaks a solemn promise made in the Lord's name, then that vow is no longer neutral but becomes a

matter of taking the Lord's name in vain (Second Commandment). A broken vow or covenant of love hinders the gracious working of God in peoples' lives and can be destructive to faith. An example of a freely made covenant is the case of congregations who bind themselves to one another in the formation of a synod or church body. If some congregations or pastors refuse to honor the agreements that they made with each other before God, then the door is potentially opened for great harm to come against God's faithful people in their church body.

Day 2 • Numbers 33; skim Deuteronomy 1–4; 9–11

6. Numbers 33 lists the places where the children of Israel set up camp for extended periods of time during their forty years of wilderness wandering. If they took several days to journey somewhere, those overnight campsites are not listed. In writing this log, Moses takes care to remind the Israelites, especially this new generation, that God has led them this far and will see them through to their inheritance in the Promised Land. This is especially important at this point in the journey because Moses himself will not be accompanying the people across the Jordan River into Canaan.

7. Deuteronomy 6 includes the "creed" of Old Testament believers, known as the *shema* (v. 4): "Hear, O Israel: the Lord our God, the Lord is one." Moses' words in this chapter impress upon the parents, especially fathers, that they must instruct their children in the Word of God so that it would never leave their minds. Although the later children of Israel literally tied words to their bodies in response to this command, its spirit of constantly remembering the Lord's teaching is certainly most important. As believers recall all that God has done for them and for former generations, they are invigorated by His promise that He will always be with them to bless them, so long as they continue to believe.

8. Deuteronomy is almost completely an extended quote from Moses. The repeated history that it contains is told from his perspective, even though it is still the inspired Word of God. It is a sermon or instruction for Israel to be careful to remember what the Lord has done for them in times past so that they continue to trust in Him for what lies before them in the land of their inheritance.

9. Originally one long book, First and Second Chronicles retell the history of Israel from Adam to the return from Babylonian exile (when it was written), emphasizing the reign of King David and temple worship. Chronicles refers back to already recorded events, presenting them as lessons in how God's hand works in each. The description of the reign of King Manasseh is strikingly different in 2 Kings and 2 Chronicles. The latter version includes the repentance and restoration of this evil king in order to bring attention to the abundant and patient grace of God for His people who sin against Him. In the retelling of the Ten Commandments, Moses emphasizes in Deuteronomy how fearful it was for the people to be so close to God's almighty presence, and how the covenant is no longer with the deceased generation, but is now the Lord's covenant with the present one.

10. Answers may vary. Several psalms may be consulted as examples. In Psalm 78, the "testimony" (v. 5) in Israel is expanded to recall several events in the exodus and the people's wandering years. It comments with specific emphasis that God's punishments were evoked because of the Israelites' lack of faith ("they forgot," "they did not remember," "did not trust," "they tested God," etc.). Psalms 105 and 106 also refer to events in Exodus and Numbers—Psalm 105, however, skips from the manna and water from the rock past all the other events of the forty years of wandering to the time when Israel entered into Canaan; Psalm 106 includes a few of these events and brings out the theme of God's servants intervening to stave off divine anger, just as Christ our Savior stood in the way of the Lord's just wrath and won eternal righteousness for all believers.

Day 3 • Numbers 34–36; Deuteronomy 19–20; 26

11. The land of Canaan, once its current inhabitants are driven out, will be divided among the tribes in proportion to the population of each tribe as of the latest census—the one taken in Numbers 26. Larger tribes will receive greater areas of land, smaller tribes will settle in smaller sections, to be preserved perpetually in their name, thanks to the year of jubilee. As was already pointed out, Reuben and Gad and the half-tribe of Manasseh will be excluded from this allotment since they will inhabit the eastern lands.

12. Property landmarks denote God-given boundaries for a family's land inheritance. Moving one of these would take away land from one neighbor and count it in favor of the other neighbor. This is not only dishonest toward one's fellow man, but it is also an offense against the Lord, drawing down one of His curses. An-

swers may vary on comparing this to today: fraud, theft, or even identity theft could be suggested. In the spiritual realm, since this was especially an offense against God, corrupting a teaching of Scripture could be considered as though someone were to move the Lord's landmark.

13. Members of the tribe of Levi will live only in certain cities that will be given them from each of the other tribes. Because of their holy tasks, they will be scattered among all their relatives, receiving their tithes and offering their sacrifices to the Lord as their inheritance.

14. A city of refuge is one of six cities granted to the Levites to serve as a sanctuary for someone who accidentally kills another. Since all shedding of blood may be avenged by the death of the killer (Genesis 9:6), those who are truly innocent of murder may stay inside the walls of the city of refuge until the high priest dies. If he leaves the city before that time, he risks death at the hands of the avenger. If it could be demonstrated by two or more witnesses that the man was a murderer or had anger against the victim or used an instrument that could cause death, then not even a city of refuge could spare him from the death penalty.

15. As the Gospel has surpassed the Law, so a gift from the generosity of a heart made free from the Law's accusations is truly preferable to that which is to be handed over upon demand. Some may point out that because of the reluctance of the sinful flesh to follow the gentle urgings of the Spirit, a required tithe would produce greater results. However, in that case, the "cheerful giver" that is pleasing to the Lord (2 Corinthians 9:7) would be nowhere to be seen. Share ideas for cultivating an improved attitude of stewardship, balancing on one hand, our obligation to the Lord to care for the resources that come from His hand alone, and on the other hand, the wonderful privilege in the Gospel's freedom to use what we have in joyful service of God's kingdom until Christ returns in glory. Especially in this matter, the Gospel needs to predominate at all times.

Day 4 • Leviticus 26–27; Deuteronomy 21; 27–29

16. These chapters are comprised of blessings that God promises to shower upon His people if they follow His Word and obey His commandments and curses that He warns would befall Israel if they despise them and break the covenant. The list of blessings and curses comes near the end of the liturgical instructions in Leviticus and just before Moses concludes his final speech on the plains of Moab, as recorded in Deuteronomy. This section can be seen as an expansion upon what the Small Catechism calls "The Close of the Commandments."

17. There are five distinct stages of admonition that the Lord will use to chastise His chosen people if they abhor His Word and break His commandments. First, God will "set [His] face" against Israel, and there will be panic, disease, and defeat from enemies. Second, a sevenfold discipline is threatened if they refuse to repent after the first stage. This is marked especially by the land itself refusing to yield its strength. Third, God will continue striking them and will let loose the wild beasts that will devour livestock and even children. Fourth, if stubborn faithlessness persists, then God will "walk contrary" to the Israelites, which is to say that His unrelenting policy will be to strike them constantly, out of vengeance for the covenant that is being savaged. Fifth, and finally, after pestilence, defeat, terror, and famine have done nothing to turn the people back to the Lord, He will strike back in fury, decimating the people, devastating the land, and removing the survivors into exile.

18. At the end of Deuteronomy 21, there is a distinctive curse addressed against anyone who is hanged on a tree. While a shameful example will be made of any criminal deserving of death, this provision in the Mosaic Law points us forward in faith to what later took place for the salvation of the world, when Jesus was lifted up on the tree of the cross. He submitted to that curse (Galatians 3:13) so that the curse our sin had deserved would be lifted from us. In Christ, we have the promise of God's eternal blessing instead.

19. The Amens in Deuteronomy 27 do not mean the people are praying! They are saying "let it be so" in response to a series of curses that will befall them if they break the covenant in the specific ways listed. Instead of its normal use, either demonstrating faith in the Lord's desire to hear and answer prayer or indicating that a gift has been received, the response "Amen" here accepts the curse and pronounces it on the people, who know full well the dire consequences of disobedience. This is analogous to placing one's hand on the Bible when taking an oath in court to tell the truth.

20. A "root bearing poisonous or bitter fruit" is a false believer who outwardly agrees with God's Word but inwardly is a stubborn opponent to the truth. Since it is a disposition of the heart, only God can identify this for certain, but there are signs that the Church and its human leaders can note and respond accordingly. This attitude can manifest itself in many ways, but if left to

fester, can cause great spiritual damage to that person and to the rest of the congregation. While a person's previous history, chemical imbalance, or emotional trauma can provide a small window into why he or she would respond to the Gospel with hatred, these psychological categories do not sufficiently explain the deeper evil that is also going on. God's Word will be resisted in this world as long as the present age lasts, even among those who once seemed to be part of the Church (1 John 2:19).

Day 5 • Deuteronomy 30–34

21. The commandment that Moses says is "not too hard" is to put simple trust in the Word of the Lord. It is not a matter of our pulling off a great feat (such as ascending to heaven or going to the depths of the sea) in order to earn God's grace and favor—those are freely given. It remains true that it is impossible for us to fulfill God's commandments perfectly; however, faith in Christ, as Paul points out to the Romans, is granted to the one who confesses Him as Lord.

22. The Song of Moses in Deuteronomy 32 is intended to convict the Israelites once they stray from the Lord's covenant. Their children in future generations will learn this song, in which they are called upon as witnesses against their forebears. Once the time of chastisement comes upon the people, they will understand the reason why God allowed it to befall them, so that then they will return to the Lord for His mercy upon Israel.

23. Answers may vary. Judah, who was granted high distinction in Jacob's blessing, receives only a few lines from Moses. In Genesis, Jacob uses more animal comparisons in his words, while in Deuteronomy, Moses tends to focus on each tribe's role in the new land.

24. At Jesus' transfiguration, Moses appeared with Elijah and Jesus and discussed His departure (Greek: *exodos*), that is, His cross and resurrection by which He would save all people. So, on the mountain in Israel, many centuries after his death, Moses finally appears in the Promised Land, which has been fulfilled in Christ. It is a bit anticlimactic for him; Luke reports that he "appeared in glory" (9:31), which seems to say that Moses has already received the blessing of heaven and was awaiting the Last Day's resurrection which is a greater blessing than it would have been to step across the Jordan River.

25. Answers may vary. Encourage responses from the group and allow some time for peole to reflect on what they will take home with them after this study. You may prompt answers by emphasizing the importance of faith in the Gospel of God's salvation rather than demanding reliance on our own works of the Law.